AF540511

RETHINKING NUCLEAR POWER

Nuclear Electricity and Nuclear Weapons Proliferation

Risto Isomäki

RETHINKING NUCLEAR POWER
Nuclear Electricity and Nuclear Weapons Proliferation
Risto Isomäki

First Published 2016

ISBN 978-93-5002-423-2

Published by
AAKAR BOOKS
28 E Pocket IV, Mayur Vihar Phase I, Delhi 110 091
Phone: 011 2279 5505 Telefax: 011 2279 5641
aakarbooks@gmail.com; www.aakarbooks.com

Laser Typeset at
Arpit Printographers, Delhi 110 032

Printed at
Saurabh Printers Pvt. Ltd., New Delhi

Contents

Foreword

Re-fashioning itself as a clean and green solition to the undeniable climate change risk is the newest strategy that the global nuclear lobby has adopted to avoid the terminal crisis it has been facing after the Fukushima disaster in Japan. A global shift away from nuclear energy primarily owing to the adverse economics and insurmountable risks of nuclear power, a decisive decline in the popular support in most countries and a sharp growth in the efficiency and competitiveness of the renewable technologies on the other hand has precipitated the crisis of the nuclear power industry. The COP21 in Paris recently saw such desperate moves to club nuclear power as part of the solution. This volume is an essential read for developing a critical perspective in this regard.

This book is an extremely useful and timely addition to the knowledge on nuclear power and its politics. In the 5th year of the ongoing Fukushima accident and the 30th year of Chernobyl disaster, Risto Isomäki highlights the inescapable dangerous inherent in the technology, dwells upon the larger asymmetries of human societies in dealing with catastrophes of nuclear kind, and refutes all the major claims of the industry on its own turf.

India is one of the very few countries embarking on

massive expansion of nuclear power in complete denial of the lessons of Fukushima. The nuclear plans, enjoying bipartisan political support, are more of a giveaway that the Indian elite has found agreeable in exchange for the international legitimisation of its nuclear weapons, than a product of some national consensus on the country's energy future. In pursuit of such highly anachronistic pipedream, the Indian state has been bulldozing all voices of dissent, views of independent experts and larger legitimate conerns regarding destruction of livelihoods and fragile ecologies. The inherently unsafe nuclear safety acquires much more lethal character in India owing to the non-independence of the nuclear regulator, non-existing safety culture and accountability, the attempts to dilute even the extremely limited legal provisions to hold nuclear suppliers liable and the general administrative corruption and apathy.

We hope that this volume by the eminent author generates wider discussion in India and at the international level.

Kumar Sundaram
Coalition for Nuclear Disarmament and Peace
(CNDP)

Preface: Why This Book?

Many high-profile environmental activists and climate scientists have recently converted from opponents of nuclear power to its eager proponents. People like James Hansen, James Lovelock Richard Rhodes, George Monbiot and Mark Lynas have said that we should perhaps also use nuclear power to prevent a global climate catastrophe, because nuclear power only produces very small carbon dioxide emissions and no soot and other suspended particles dangerous to our health.

These ideas are very familiar for me and I can easily understand and sympathize with the concerns expressed by the above mentioned persons, for whom I have always greatly respect.

My own journey has proceeded in the opposite direction.

I was, myself, an eager proponent of nuclear power during the years 1978-1982. I preached that we should invest more in nuclear power because it does not produce greenhouse gas emissions, acid rain or dangerous particulate emissions, and because the radioactive emissions of coal and peat fired power plants were much larger than those from nuclear power plants.

All this was and still is true. However, I soon became sceptical about the economics of nuclear power and started to think that it is stupid to invest practically all governmental research and development funds aiming to develop new energy sources in nuclear power. This was like putting all our eggs in the same basket, which is not generally considered as the wise thing to do. Somewhat later, I also started to question the safety of nuclear power from a number of different viewpoints and the more I learned the more worried I became.

Now, after thirty-five years as a science and science fiction writer and science journalist—and approximately two million science reports, excerpts and summaries later —I am convinced that nuclear technologies are an even greater risk for humanity's long-term survival than the terrifying double threat of global warming and ocean acidification.

The following pages are an effort to explain why I have arrived at such a conclusion. Many of the things I have mentioned are probably familiar for most people who have been studying the problems related to nuclear power but some might be new because they are based on less well known sources or non-published discussions with nuclear physicists.

The first chapter explains why nuclear weapons might still be much more dangerous than what we have understood. This may sound like a sick joke because everybody knows that nuclear bombs are hugely destructive, but I think that the issue is of utmost importance. The Hiroshima and Nagasaki bombs were exploded in small towns but they still created huge firestorms and hurricane-strength winds blowing towards them. Even a small nuclear weapon detonated in a large modern city would probably do much more damage than we have this far acknowledged.

Chapter two concentrates on the two main mechanisms through which even our present uranium reactors assist the spread of nuclear weapons to new countries: the production of plutonium and the dissemination of gas centrifuges that can also be used to make nuclear weapons.

The third chapter explains why problems related to nuclear proliferation will get out of control if we also start to construct thorium reactors or other breeder reactors, also known as fourth-generation nuclear reactors.

Chapter four discusses what we do know and what we do not yet know about the health effects of radioactive exposures, and why we may have underestimated the impact of certain types of radioactive pollution.

The last four chapters analyse how much radioactivity could be released from nuclear power complexes in different worst case scenarios, whether fusion might finally bring us safe and clean nuclear power and whether we really need nuclear electricity to prevent a greenhouse catastrophe.

In a way I would say that I started writing this book already during the summer of 1980. I had just finished my school and working in a regional newspaper. I went to cover an International Atomic Energy Association's working group meeting that was held in Hotel Tallukka in Vääksy, in Central Finland.

Two highly respected international nuclear gurus agreed to give me an interview. They started by outlining their views about the subjects that had been discussed at the meeting. When they had stopped I said: "Look, I am on your side, I am strongly pro-nuclear, you don't have to behave like this. I only know school book physics but even I know that the things you just told me contained at least fourteen mistakes or misleading half-truths."

Smiles disappeared from the faces of the highly esteemed nuclear experts. They looked at me as if I was a piece of cheap sausage and thanked me for the interview.

After the "interview", I was still pro-nuclear but had an uncomfortable feeling about not being told everything. Because I wanted to know the whole truth, I started to investigate and I am still digging, because knowledge about nuclear technologies is like an enormous onion. You peel off layer after layer but still, thirty-five years later, you discover issues in which you have been cheated and misled.

Helsinki **Risto Isomäki**
4th January 2016

1

How Destructive are Nuclear Weapons?

All the safety and public health issues discussed in this book are relevant and deserve wider public attention than what they have, this far, received. However, the most important problem related to nuclear power is and will always be the danger of spreading nuclear weapons and nuclear weapons technology to numerous new countries.

Nuclear weapons proliferation may be an even more serious threat for humanity's long-term survival than global warming. According to new studies nuclear weapons seem to be even more destructive than we have assumed.

This is because nuclear bombs are, in essence, huge fire-bombs. Roughly one half of their energy is released as electromagnetic radiation. The energy of the blast or the pressure wave of an explosion weakens quickly with the distance because its energy is released into space with three dimensions. The destructive capacity of electromagnetic radiation, on the other hand, decreases as a square root of distance. With it the key factor is how much radiation falls on a square centimeter of surface. s a thumb rule, areas that receive the minimum of 10 calories of energy for square centimetre of surface in the form of electromagnetic radiation are consumed by fire because numerous separate fires ignited by the radiation grow together and produce a mega-fire known as a firestorm.

In Hiroshima and Nagasaki nuclear detonations caused firestorms which burned everything and killed everybody inside the fire perimeter.

In spite of this the US Military considered fire damage so unpredictable, that for fifty years they only concentrated in analysing the impact of the blast, or the pressure wave caused by the nuclear detonation. Military scientists spent a huge effort to measure, very carefully, the force vectors caused by nuclear detonations. They measured how many millimetres a nail was pushed inside a beam within varying distances from Ground Zero by the pressure wave. At the same time they removed all that could burn like plastics, wood and paper from their experimental houses and villages that were to be destroyed by the blasts. There were no inflammable furniture and the curtains were made of metal sheets. In other words, to find out precisely enough how much destruction the pressure wave of a nuclear explosion could do, an extreme effort was made to ensure that the experimental houses or anything inside them could not ignite and burn. Fires might have distorted the results!

The US military spent at least USD 5,500 billion in the development of its nuclear weapons systems and constructed a nuclear arsenal equivalent to 1,600,000 Hiroshima bombs largely because of this approach: because it hugely underestimated the destructive potential of firestorms ignited by nuclear explosions.

The story has been documented by Lynn Eden, Associate Director for Research at the Center for International Security and Cooperation in Stanford University, USA. Eden's very important book, *Whole World on Fire, Organizations, Knowledge and Nuclear Weapons Devastation* makes sobering reading and should be disseminated more widely.

When the USA was afraid of a major military conflict between Pakistan and India in 2002, it warned that a nuclear war in South Asia might kill twelve million people. The figure was absurdly low, because it only took the impact of the nuclear blasts (pressure waves) into consideration. According to more recent US research fire damage radii of nuclear blasts are 2 to 5 times larger than those determined for airblast effects. In practice this means, that areas destroyed by firestorms ignited by nuclear detonations are 4 to 25 times larger than areas damaged by blast, alone.

Unfortunately, even this is not yet the full picture. The firestorms in Dresden, Hamburg, Hiroshima and Nagasaki caused very strong rising air currents, which in turn created hurricane-strength winds, blowing with speeds from 160 to 270 kilometres per hour towards the firestorm. A nuclear explosion in a modern city would create a still fiercer firestorm because our cities now contain huge quantities of hydrocarbons in the form of plastics, asphalt, gasoline, oil and gas. A firestorm in a modern city would create phenomenal, super-hurricane winds.

It has been estimated that even the explosion of a small, Hiroshima-size nuclear bomb in Manhattan created winds blowing with the speed of 600 kilometres per hour towards the firestorm. Such a super-hurricane was strong enough to topple skyscrapers and to destroy most other human-made structures, in an area dozens of times larger than the area destroyed by the firestorm and up to one thousand times larger than the area devastated by the original nuclear blast.

For example, the high skyscrapers of Manhattan have been designed to withstand 250-kilometres-per hour winds without toppling, but the force vectors created by a 600-kilometres-per hour wind would be more than ten times stronger.

Insurance companies have estimated that the destructive potential of wind increases 650 per cent when the wind speed increases from 20-26 metres per second to 26-31 metres per second. What kind of devastation was produced by wind speeds approaching 200 metres per second?

Such super-hurricane winds might perhaps give birth to thousands, if not millions, of secondary fires, which might grow together and produce new firestorms. A wind blowing 600 kilometres per hour can throw cars, buses, lorries and motorcycles around, so that their fuel tanks burst. Metal hitting on metal, power lines felled by the winds and all kinds of things being thrown around and acting as projectiles can produce sparks. Gas pipes breaking inside collapsing houses and shattering fireplaces would cause many fires. There would be a huge amount of static electricity in the air, caused by the dry wind, dust and sand. If the event took place during a bush and forest fire season, millions of burning trees could act as firebrands.

This means that we may not need a huge, full-scale nuclear war—in which hundreds or thousands of nuclear bombs are used—to trigger the feared nuclear winter, a scenario in which the dust and soot from nuclear detonations blocked a major part of sunlight and froze the earth by causing a 30 or 50 degree Celsius drop in global average temperatures. A few dozen nuclear weapons detonated inside large cities might be enough to cause a nuclear winter, if they produced huge firestorms that burned enormous areas to ashes.

According to studies conducted by Alan Robock, of the

Rutgers University, and Owen B. Toon of the University of Colorado at Boulder, for example a relatively small nuclear war between Pakistan and India could have major global consequences. If both countries launched 50 Hiroshima-sized warheads, the ensuing firestorms might produce seven million tons of smoke, and cool the planet so much that many crops would fail. According to Robock and Toon such an exchange of 100 nuclear weapons between Pakistan and India would probably cause a global famine, killing about one billion people. In the light of the things mentioned above, this sounds like a relatively moderate estimate. The truth could be much worse.

According to another recent study one or two megaton nuclear war fought with one hundred or so Hiroshima-sized nuclear bombs in northern sub-tropical cities might destroy a major part of the stratospheric ozone layer which protects us from the deadly ultraviolet-C (or UVC) radiation. If we lose the ozone layer, the incoming ultraviolet light's ability to burn our eyes and skin increases roughly 30-fold. UVC radiation would also do serious damage for our food crops and plankton.

Even a single nuclear weapon might cause a world-wide disaster, if it was directed against a very dangerous target.

March 15, 1968 the Soviet nuclear submarine K-129 exploded near the main island of Hawaii. The US military saw the explosion, and later raised parts of the vessel. They discovered that the fuel of a missile equipped with a one-megaton warhead had exploded and the detonation sunk the submarine. The scariest thing was that the hatch of the missile silo had evidently been open when the explosion happened. If the hatch had been closed during the explosion, the pressure wave would have torn it away. However, the hatch was still there, which was only possible if it had already been open when the submarine was destroyed by the exploding fuel. The best explanation for these facts was that K-129 had tried to launch at least one nuclear missile towards Pearl Harbour.

It was later found that the Soviet High Command had, some weeks earlier, lost contact with K-129. Even more strangely, the submarine had carried out a number of odd manoeuvres which were not technically necessary for it but which would, at that time, have been necessary for the military submarines of China.

One of the theories put forward to explain what happened is that the commander of K-129, KGB or a section of the KGB had decided to attack Pearl Harbour, in order to trigger a nuclear war between China and the USA, to ease the more and more difficult strategic position of the Soviet Union.

The theory may sound far-fetched, but the story of K-129 has been documented in detail. I have mentioned a few key books and other references at the end of this volume. You can study them and decide yourself what to think about it. In any case, K-129 probably is the most hair-raising of all the numerous terrifying Cold War stories!

If a one-megaton nuclear weapon had detonated in Pearl Harbour, in the middle of thousands of nuclear bombs and hundreds of small nuclear reactors powering nuclear submarines and other warships, the ensuing radioactive fallout would have killed very many people on every continent. Not to say what would have happened if the event had triggered a full-scale nuclear war between China and the USA. As mentioned above, the combined nuclear weapons potential of the USA at the time was equivalent to 1,600,000 Hiroshima bombs.

An even worse possibility would be the so-called Gorbachev-Reagan-scenario.

After the Chernobyl accident, Mikhail Gorbachev started to worry of what would happen, if somebody attacked a nuclear power plant complex with a nuclear weapon. Gorbachev spoke about his concerns to Ronald Reagan's security adviser, who reported the matter to Reagan. Reagan later described the story in his memoirs.

This might still be the worst-case scenario. A nuclear weapon, especially one producing many neutrons (like uranium-lithium-deuteride bomb, see the following chapters) would vaporize the reactors and transform their contents into an almost unimaginably lethal radoactive cloud. The fissile materials in the nuclear power plant might strenghten the power of the explosion, if the original nuclear explosions produced a large enough amount of neutrons.

At the moment the risk of such an occurrence is very small, but if we do not eliminate our remaining nuclear arsenals but let our nuclear experts spread nuclear technology to a hundred new countries, it becomes almost inevitable that something very nasty will finally happen, sooner or later.

The Dark Angel Scenario

There is one more issue that ought to be mentioned, here. During the Cold War, the US military realized that a single, relatively large nuclear weapon detonated high above the United States, at the height of 20 kilometres or so, would create an extremely strong electromagnetic pulse (EMP).

Such a huge EMP was strong enough to fry all unprotected electronic equipment, including computers, throughout the continental USA. This is again because roughly one half of a nuclear bomb's energy is released in the form of electromagnetic radiation.

Since then the risks have multiplied because power transmission lines have become longer and because many apartment and office buildings—especially large company headquarters—have connected hundreds of computers together via internal cable systems, intranets. From the viewpoint of an EMP intranet systems and long transmission lines are like super-large, super-efficient antennas that can capture a lot of energy from the pulse and then concentrate it on the vulnerable parts of computers and servers.

In other words, a single nuclear weapon could destroy the whole electronic infrastructure, power grids, internet, mobile phone networks and computers on a continent-wide area.

The EMP commission, the official expert committee of the US Congress investigating the matter, estimated that if a one-megaton nuclear weapon were detonated 160 kilometres above the continental USA, between 70 and more than 90 per cent of the US population would die during the first year after the incident, meaning 200 or 300 million people.

This sounds impossible, but the EMP created by such a detonation would fry everything electric within the line of sight, unless it had been "hardened", meaning protected from an EMP. At the moment everything in the USA functions with electricity, practically nothing has been protected against an EMP and everything is within a line of sight if the detonation takes place 160 kilometres above the ground.

After such an event the water would soon run out because the pumps filling the water towers would not operate. People in the cities would run out of drinking water and they would not be able to flush their toilets. Cities would have to be abandoned. The water and wastewater treatment facilities would not work and pure drinking water would soon run out. The whole food system—agriculture and distribution—of the USA depends on electric equipment, so the food would also run out soon, as well as medicines and vaccines. It would not be possible to heat the houses during winter and all kinds of epidemics would soon become rampant. A 90 per cent mortality within one year sounds realistic, if not optimistic.

A similar event over Europe might cause up to 800 million fatalities because Europe is equally vulnerable than the USA and has many more people packed into the same area of land.

And what could happen if India and the other South Asian countries followed the lead of Europe and the USA and made themselves as dependent on electricity, without protecting their electric grids against an EMP? If this became a reality, a single nuclear detonation over South Asia in 2080 could kill up to three billion people in the region and produce a huge wave of pandemics eating their way over the planet. Besides this, the nuclear installations constructed on the coastal areas of South Asian countries would lose the power of their cooling systems with the grid, but I will return to this problem, somewhat later in this book.

I have been calling such an event the Dark Angel scenario, according to a ground-breaking TV series that also made the US-Mexican actress Jessica Alba a big star. The events of the series took place in the ruins of a world destroyed by an EMP produced by a single nuclear weapon, detonated 130 kilometres above the surface of the earth.

Something like this could really happen, one day, unless we begin to take the dangers related to nuclear technology more seriously. Whatever we do, it is of crucial importance that we will protect the key parts of our electric grids, health care systems and the factories producing vaccines, medicines, water purification chemicals and fertilizers against an EMP. "Hardening" electric equipment against an EMP increases the costs of production from 3 to 10 per cent and by hardening something like 10 per cent of all the equipment (in the key facilities mentioned above) a major catastrophe can be avoided even if the worst would become true and a rogue state or a terrorist organization would detonate a nuclear weapon above South Asia, China, Europe or the USA.

2

Nuclear Power and Nuclear Weapons Proliferation: Ordinary Nuclear Reactors

All the atoms belonging to the same element like carbon, iron or uranium contain the same number of protons in their nucleus. The number of protons defines the chemical properties of an atom. The nuclei, however, also contain another type of heavy sub-atomic particles, neutrons. The number of neutrons can differ even in the atoms that belong to the same element. Two atoms that contain a similar number of protons but a different number of neutrons belong to the same element. They are called isotopes of that element.

For instance, uranium atoms always contain 92 protons, but uranium 235 also contains 143 neutrons. Uranium 238 contains 92 protons and 146 neutrons, and so on.

In a way it could be said that every element is a family of isotopes, some of which exist naturally and some of which can be produced in nuclear reactors or by nuclear detonations, by bombarding the atomic nuclei with neutrons so that they are captured by the nuclei.

Even though the isotopes of the same element have similar chemical characteristics, their radioactive properties can be dramatically different. Some isotopes are stable, meaning they are not radioactive. Some isotopes are mildly radioactive which means that they decay and split into other elements only very slowly, while some isotopes are highly radioactive.

What comes to nuclear weapons, the important isotopes are uranium 233 and uranium 235 and all the isotopes of plutonium. A one-stage nuclear weapon or the first stage of a two- or three-stage nuclear weapon has to be made of plutonium or of uranium containing the minimum of 10 per cent of uranium 233 or the minimum of 20 per cent of uranium 235.

Because the fuel of our present nuclear power plants only contains 0.7–3.6 per cent of uranium 235 it cannot be used, as such, to manufacture nuclear weapons. However, even our conventional nuclear power plants have two serious problems from the viewpoint of nuclear weapons proliferation: they produce plutonium when they are operating and the technology that is used in the production (enrichment) of their fuel can also be used to produce raw material for uranium bombs.

The latter problem arises because the so-called weapons grade uranium and nuclear fuel are both produced by exactly similar—by the same—gas centrifuges. The only difference is, that if you want to make a nuclear bomb (and have uranium in which the uranium 235 content has been enriched to 20-93 per cent) instead of producing fuel for nuclear reactors (in which the uranium 235 content has been enriched to the maximum of 3.6 per cent) you have to install a longer series of gas centrifuges or run the gas via the same shorter series of centrifuges very many times.

The important point is to understand, that the difference between nuclear and nuclear reactor technology is a line drawn in water. We are, in essence, talking about the same thing. Ted Taylor, one of the most important nuclear weapons designers of the USA remarked that the spectrum between reactors and bombs is a continuum and there is very little difference between a runaway nuclear reactor and a fizzling nuclear bomb.

Three Routes to Nuclear Weapons

When a country wants to acquire nuclear weapons, it has to choose between three alternative routes. One is plutonium, one is uranium 235 and one is uranium 233.

If access to suitable materials is not a problem, a uranium bomb is technically easier to make than a plutonium bomb.

Plutonium atoms are easier to split than uranium atoms, but there is a catch. If you want to produce a proper nuclear detonation from plutonium, you have to compress it with equal force from all directions, simultaneously. In other words, you need to produce a symmetrical implosion, an explosion whose energy is directed inwards. Achieving something like this caused problems for the scientists who constructed the first nuclear weapons during the Second World War. In our own time producing a symmetrical implosion would still be somewhat challenging for most terrorist organizations—but not for governments.

Uranium bombs can be exploded without producing a symmetrical explosion. If you have uranium that contains at least 20 per cent uranium 235 or, alternatively, at least 10 per cent uranium 233, you can just divide your uranium into two parts, and shoot the smaller part towards the larger one with conventional explosives in a metal tube. This kind of a tube bomb (the Hiroshima bomb) is the simplest possible nuclear weapon.

The higher the proportion of the fissile uranium 233 or

uranium 235, the smaller amount of material is needed in order to make a nuclear weapon. If you have so-called weapons grade uranium that contains 93 per cent of uranium 235 and 7 per cent of uranium 238, you need slightly less than 20 kilograms in order to make a Hiroshima bomb. If your uranium only contains 20 per cent of uranium 235 and 80 per cent of uranium 238, you need 400 kilograms to achieve a similar destructive capacity. On the other hand, if you had (almost) pure uranium 235, you would only need 270 grams of the stuff to produce a small but powerful nuclear weapon. Uranium 233 atoms split easier, so with it even smaller amounts and purities are needed.

Luckily, natural uranium contains only 0.7 per cent of uranium 235 and 99.3 per cent of uranium 238, and almost no uranium 233. This means that you cannot, in practice, make a nuclear weapon of natural uranium without first enriching (increasing) the proportion of uranium 235 in it. Or, to be more precise, you cannot make the first or second stage of a nuclear weapon from natural uranium. We come back to this, later.

It is not easy to alter the proportions of the different isotopes of the same element. This is because they are chemically similar and cannot thus be separated by the means provided by chemistry. During the Second World War, Germany led the world in natural sciences, including physics and chemistry. In spite of this, Hitler's scientists were only able to increase the uranium 235 content from 0.7 per cent to 1.5 per cent in 1 gram of uranium hexafluoride gas, between September 1939 and March 1941. This wasn't very much, because they would have needed either 20 kilograms of uranium containing 93 per cent or 400 kilograms of uranium containing 20 per cent of uranium 235 to make a Hiroshima bomb. So the Nazi scientists never got close to producing a nuclear weapon.

Plutonium, on the other hand, can be separated from uranium chemically, and every nuclear reactor using uranium manufactures plutonium as its by-product. Yes, this is correct: even every civilian nuclear reactor on our planet also makes raw material for nuclear weapons, every day it operates. Every second it operates.

An average-sized nuclear reactor produces about 30 tons of used nuclear fuel in a year. Every ton contains 1-2 per cent or 10-20 kilograms of plutonium.

As mentioned above, you have to be able to produce a symmetrical implosion in order to achieve a plutonium explosion. This is the easier the more plutonium 239 (and the less plutonium 240) your plutonium contains.

When a nuclear reactor begins to operate, a great majority of the plutonium being generated is plutonium 239. The longer the reactor operates, the larger part of the plutonium 239 becomes converted to plutonium 240 by the neutron bombardment. The plutonium in used nuclear fuel typically contains 65-70 per cent of plutonium 239 and most of the rest is plutonium 240. This kind of a mixture of plutonium isotopes is known as "reactor plutonium".

It has often been claimed in newspaper stories that reactor plutonium cannot be used to make nuclear weapons. This is not correct. The claim is a remnant from the Cold War. The idea has its origins in the disinformation fed to the public by the governments of the nuclear powers, but it has persisted even long after the US government and other Western governments had publicly admitted that they had been lying to the public on this issue.

The fact that you can make a nuclear weapon from

reactor plutonium containing 65 to 70 per cent of plutonium 239 was declassified in the USA in 1977. It received widespread attention when the US Secretary for Energy Hazel O'Leary revealed in a press conference that the USA had made and detonated a nuclear bomb made of reactor plutonium already in 1962.

For example, the first crude nuclear weapons detonated by North Korea were most probably made of reactor plutonium. The more advanced nuclear powers prefer to use so-called weapons grade plutonium or plutonium that contains at least 93 per cent of plutonium 239.

Unlike uranium, all the isotopes of plutonium are fissile and easy to split. This means that all of them can be used in nuclear weapons, all isotopes and all conceivable mixtures of them. According to some experts the only exception to this main rule might be plutonium that contains so much (more than 80 per cent) plutonium 238 that it would be next to impossible to prevent the cocktail from overheating.

However, the making of a plutonium bomb is the easier the smaller the share of plutonium 240 is. The decay of plutonium 240 produces slow neutrons that can spoil the explosion by causing the weapon to self-detonate a little bit too early. If this happens, the weapon only achieves 10 or 20 per cent of its explosive potential. This is also why you need an implosion to detonate a plutonium bomb!

The problem is only relative because all plutonium always contains some plutonium 240. In weapons grade plutonium 66 wrong kinds of neutrons per second are generated in each gram, while reactor plutonium produces 360 problematic neutrons per gram per second.

Plutonium 241 also causes its own complications because it decays to americium 241 which is a bit too radioactive for convenience. Because of the gamma radiation from americium it is more dangerous and tricky to handle plutonium that contains a lot of plutonium 241. And, as I already mentioned, plutonium 238 produces a lot of heat.

Unfortunately all these problems can be overcome, relatively easily. If a government has plutonium, it can make a nuclear weapon. This means that every country that has even one nuclear reactor should be classified as a country that possesses nuclear weapons capacity, an ability to make nuclear bombs at short notice. Even if it has not made any nuclear weapons, yet, it could do so very quickly if it one day changed its mind. It would only be a matter of days, weeks or months, depending on the technical capacity of the country in question. Even North Korea only needed less than a year.

Besides, if you store your nuclear fuel, the plutonium in it improves with time.

The half-lives of the key isotopes of plutonium are as follows:

Pu 238	87.7 years
Pu 239	24,100 years
Pu 240	6,563 years
Pu 241	14.4 years

During the half-life of an isotope, one half of its atoms decay and change to something else. This means that the overall amount is reduced to one half during one half-life, and to one quarter in two.

The isotope that is best suited for making nuclear weapons (plutonium 239) has a much longer half-life than the three somewhat problematic isotopes (plutonium 238, plutonium 240 and plutonium 241).

This means that the plutonium 239 content in the used

nuclear fuel becomes gradually larger. The plutonium kind of enriches itself, spontaneously, first from reactor grade plutonium to weapons grade plutonium (containing 93 per cent of plutonium 239) and then to ultra-grade plutonium (containing 97 or 98 per cent of plutonium 239) and finally to (almost) pure plutonium 239 that can be detonated like the uranium bomb, without the need to produce a symmetrical explosion.

Two- and Three-Staged Nuclear Weapons

I have said, on the preceding pages, that you can only make a nuclear weapon from plutonium or from uranium containing at least 10 per cent uranium 233 or at least 20 per cent of uranium 235, or from a mixture of these isotopes.

This is the main rule. However, it only applies to the first stage of a nuclear weapon. You cannot have a nuclear weapon without the above-mentioned materials because you cannot have a two- or three-stage nuclear weapon without the first stage. But if you have the materials for the first stage, you can also make much larger two- or three-stage weapons in which natural uranium can also be used.

A two-stage nuclear weapon is called a thermonuclear weapon, a hydrogen bomb or a fission-fusion bomb. A three-stage weapon is called a hydrogen-uranium bomb or a fission-fusion-fission bomb. All these terms are somewhat misleading and simplify things considerably. In reality the nuclear reactions taking place in a two- or three-stage nuclear weapon are extremely complicated.

But, simply put, in a thermonuclear weapon you use a small plutonium or uranium 233/235 (usually plutonium) trigger to achieve fusion of deuterium and tritium. The fusion of these two heavy isotopes of hydrogen releases much more energy than the fission of uranium or plutonium.

The destructive capacity of a thermonuclear bomb can be further magnified by adding some lithium into the mixture.

At the beginning of the 1950s it cost about 60 US cents or 0.6 dollars to add a kiloton of explosive strength to a thermonuclear weapon by adding some lithium 6 to it. Six dollars per Hiroshima. The Hungarian-American nuclear physicist Edward Teller, who together with his Polish colleague Stanislaw Ulam discovered the main principle of thermonuclear weapons, commented that why buy a cow when powdered milk is so much cheaper?

With lithium it is also possible to make three-stage nuclear weapons, in which the last stage consists of ordinary natural uranium containing 99.3 per cent uranium 238 and 0.7 per cent uranium 235. Also depleted uranium that contains 99.7 per cent uranium 238 and 0.3 per cent uranium 235 can be used.

Uranium 238 cannot normally be used in a nuclear weapon because its atoms do not split that easily and when they split the neutrons that are produced cannot split other atoms. For this reason the nuclear reactions do not accelerate but kind of fizz off if there is too much uranium 238 in the bomb, or more precisely, in the first stage of the bomb.

But if you detonate a small plutonium or uranium 233/ 235 trigger inside a mantle consisting of lithium 6 and deuterium, it is a whole different matter. When the trigger explodes, many different energy- and neutron-producing reactions take place, almost simultaneously. Litium 6 is split to tritium. Some deuterium atoms fuse with deuterium.

Other deuterium atoms fuse with tritium. All these reactions release a lot of energy and produce neutrons that can split uranium 238 atoms. The neutrons created when the uranium 238 atoms split can no longer split other uranium 238 atoms, but the flow of neutrons from the tritium-deuterium-lithium explosion is so massive that very many uranium 238 atoms split and a huge amount of energy is liberated.

If you want to build truly humongous nuclear weapons this is the way to do it. All the biggest nuclear weapons built or detonated during the Cold War were three-stage nuclear weapons whose last stage consisted of natural uranium. The largest nuclear weapon ever built was called Tsar Bomba, the Czar of bombs. It originally had an explosive capacity of a mind-boggling 100 megatons, but the Russians only exploded it, on purpose, with less than half of this strength.

With three-stage nuclear weapons there are no clear limits for how large the bomb can be. There is no upper size, because the trigger can be very small, and the second and third stages consisting of lithium-deuteride and ordinary uranium 238 or natural uranium are always stable and cannot explode without the trigger, even if the bomb has the size of a small mountain.

The nastiest characteristic of hydrogen-uranium bombs is that they do not burn cleanly but produce an exceptionally lethal radioactive cloud. They are nuclear weapons and dirty bombs in the same package. The radioactive fallout from Castle Bravo (an 11-megaton hydrogen-uranium bomb) would probably have killed all the people of a Pacific atoll situated 500 kilometres from the Ground Zero unless its inhabitants had been evacuated by the US military. This is the main reason why nobody has built any three-stage nuclear bombs after the 1960s.

However, their physics is, from the viewpoint of the 21st century, frighteningly simple. The trickiest part to obtain is the trigger, but it doesn't have to be very large. If you have very pure uranium 235, 270 grams is enough. An even smaller amount of uranium 233 would do. If you have plutonium, you probably only need a few dozens of grams of it, even though this is somewhat speculative, because the real figure is still classified.

Among the physicists there is a widespread rumour that the smallest amount of plutonium that can be used to trigger a two- or three-staged nuclear weapon is only 6 grams. I do not know and actually do not want to know whether this is true, or whether this is only a scientific urban legend.

Acquiring deuterium, lithium and natural uranium is, unfortunately, much easier. Depleted uranium can be bought, it is not a controlled substance, largely because the US weapons industry wants to sell shells and other ammunition with tips made of depleted uranium. Uranium is a very heavy element and uranium shells have a higher penetrative capacity than conventional ammunition. Besides this, depleted uranium ignites and burns when it hits something hard, like an enemy tank. This produces spectacular flashes that were extremely demoralizing for the Iraqi tank troops during the First Gulf War.

A typical nuclear power plant consumes about 30 tons of enriched uranium fuel in a year and the enrichment or production of this thirty tons produces 200 tons of depleted uranium. In other words, the world's stores of depleted uranium used to grow with the speed of 80,000 or 100,000 tons per year because we are producing electricity with nuclear power.

Deuterium can be distilled from sea water. One hydrogen atom in 6,000 in the sea water contains one atom of deuterium and one atom of ordinary hydrogen, instead of two ordinary hydrogen atoms. The water molecules that containing deuterium are slightly heavier than ordinary water molecules. They are, therefore, called heavy water or deuterized water. If you take 6,000 litres of sea water and distil 5,999 litres of it away, the last remaining litre is heavy water and contains deuterium, which can be extracted with the means of simple electrolysis (by splitting the water molecules with electric power).

How about lithium? The isotope lithium 6 works best in nuclear weapons but natural lithium that contains 7.5 per cent lithium 6 and 92.5 per cent lithium 7 can also be used. For example the lithium in the already mentioned Castle Bravo nuclear bomb, detonated by the US in the Bikini Islands on March 1, 1954, contained 40 per cent of lithium 6 and 60 per cent of lithium 7. The explosion was three times larger than the Americans had expected, because also a large part of lithium 7 atoms were split by the triggering explosion and produced neutrons that were able to split uranium 238 atoms.

This is bad news, because lithium has become a very common and important metal in the modern economy. The batteries of cell phones and computers use lithium, and the best currently existing batteries of electric cars use lithium iron phosphate. It will be next to impossible to control the availability of lithium.

If we cannot do much to reduce the availability of lithium, deuterium or natural uranium, the most important thing is to control the availability of plutonium and uranium 233/235 as strictly as possible.

This, of course, is what the world has been trying to do, with one notable exception. While we have otherwise done our utmost to restrict the availability of plutonium and uranium 233/235, we have at the same time actively and enthusiastically promoted the spread of plutonium-producing equipment (nuclear reactors) and uranium 233/235 enriching equipment (centrifuges that make nuclear fuel).

In other words, we have been acting like a schizophrenic mental case. Or like a moron, a simple person who has the average intelligence of an eight-year-old person and who can carry out simple tasks under instructions but cannot really understand the meaning or consequences of his own acts.

What To Do with the Used Nuclear Fuel?

Most countries with nuclear power plants have not yet decided what they will do with their used nuclear fuel, containing 2 or 3 per cent of plutonium, about 97 per cent of uranium and less than 1 per cent of other highly radioactive contaminants.

Finland and Sweden are the only countries which have already decided that they will bury the waste in copper containers in deep artificial cave systems excavated inside the bedrock. Finland is already constructing the world's first underground storage system for its used nuclear fuel. The cave system is called Onkalo, Onkalo being one of the words for a cave in the Finnish language.

Public debate related to Onkalo has this far concentrated on the threat caused by the buried radioactive substances for future generations. There has been a lot of talk about what kinds of markings or statues of devilish-looking monsters could warn the people living in the same area 10,000 or 100,000 years later about the dangerous materials stored inside the bedrock.

It is inevitable that some radioactive waste will, sooner or later, be released from the copper containers and that there will be a massive local groundwater contamination problem. If we store huge amount of radioactive substances inside the bedrock, local groundwater resources will inevitably become contaminated with radioactive substances, after a few hundred or a few thousand years. After this it will probably take a few tens of thousands of years or slightly longer before the local groundwater is again safe to drink.

It would be foolish to assume anything else. However, radioactive contamination of local groundwater resources is not a very important issue, in this context.

The main issue is that even after 100,000 years, the plutonium in Onkalo could still be used for making tens of thousands of Nagasaki-sized plutonium bombs or the triggers (first stages) of millions of much larger two- or three-staged nuclear weapons.

At the moment Finland is a democratic and relatively peace-loving country. However, during the last ten years it has become slightly involved with two wars: the US-led war against the Taliban in Afghanistan and in the international military operations against Somalian pirate fleets.

In 1941 Finland attacked the Soviet Union, together with Hitler's Germany, Romania, Hungary, Italy and Spain. The attack resulted in the deaths of nine million Soviet soldiers and between ten and eighteen million civilians.

In 1919-21 Finland was one of the numerous countries that attacked Russia during its bloody civil war, in order to support the various White Armies against the Red Army. These foreign interventions probably prolonged the civil war, and made it more destructive than what it had otherwise been. Partly because of the foreign interventions, the war cost the lives of 8-10 million people.

In 1918 there was a civil war in Finland. Only 6,000 people died in the fighting. But the illegal executions and other atrocities after the war probably brought the total number of deaths to something like 45,000, which was a lot, considering that Finland only had about 1.5 million inhabitants.

During the previous one hundred years, Finland was a part of the very aggressive Russian empire, and supplied its armies and navies with elite officers, generals and admirals, thus participating in dozens of colonial wars in different parts of Asia.

Before that Finland was, for six hundred years, an integral part of a military empire that was even more ruthless and aggressive than the Russian empire. Sweden was the Third Reich of the 17th century, and perhaps 20 million people died in its pitiless imperial wars, in Germany, in Poland, in Russia, in Latvia, Lithuania and Estonia, in Norway and Denmark, and elsewhere in Europe.

All this has happened in less than 800 years. Can we be sure that during the next 80,800 or 80,000 years there will be no military dictators in Finland, or that the country will not be invaded by a new Hitler, Stalin, Tamerlane, Gustavus II Adolphus or Genghis Khan?

If we cannot be sure of this, we should not bury huge

amounts of plutonium into the bedrock, into a place that the future Stalins or Hitlers would find very easily. If we do something like this, we may force the next five thousand or ten thousand generations to live in a constant fear of totalitarian regimes and mad dictators possessing nuclear weapons.

If we want to produce nuclear power, we should at least store the used nuclear fuel safely, inside the several-kilometres-thick saltbeds at the bottom of the ocean. If there is a kilometre of salt and then some mud and a few kilometres of water above the plutonium-containing nuclear waste deposits, it would be impossible for any future mass murderer to locate them. Salt layers block both electromagnetic radiation (all wavelengths) and sound waves. You cannot see through salt, with any known method! Besides this, salt automatically seals all the cracks made by earthquakes, because it behaves more like a very thick liquid than a solid.

3

Nuclear Power and Nuclear Weapons Proliferation: Breeder Reactors

The world's rich natural uranium deposits are limited. There is a vastly larger amount of uranium in the earth's crust, but mostly in very small or tiny concentrations. The richer deposits could probably provide fuel for the present number of nuclear reactors for one hundred years or so, but that's that.

In practice this means that if we want to produce much more nuclear energy, we have to shift to breeder reactors, to nuclear reactors that produce more nuclear fuel than they consume.

Breeder reactor technology would increase our economically available nuclear fuel reserves by hundreds of times, at least in theory. But this would come with a very high price.

As mentioned before, the fuel of our present nuclear reactors only contains between 0.7 and 3.6 per cent of the easily fissile uranium 235 isotope.

Breeder reactors, on the other hand, use nuclear fuels in which the percentage of fissile isotopes has been enriched to 15, 20 or 60 per cent, sometimes even more. Certain parts of the planned thorium reactors would contain almost pure uranium 233. In a nutshell: it is possible to make nuclear weapons from the fuel of a breeder reactor, even without any further enrichment.

As discussed in the preceding chapter, you can make a nuclear weapon if you have uranium that contains the minimum of 20 per cent of uranium 235 or the minimum of 10 per cent of uranium 233. Plutonium-uranium oxides that contain even less than 10 per cent of plutonium will also do, but bombs made of such stuff must be detonated with a symmetrical implosion.

It seems that the whole nuclear establishment, including the companies producing nuclear power, the companies making nuclear reactors, the science and technology institutes involved in nuclear research, the nuclear safety authorities and the International Atomic Energy Association, has already decided that we will soon move from the ordinary nuclear reactors to breeder reactors. They see this as a given, something that has already happened, something that is natural and inevitable, something that is beneficial for the human kind. They no longer question, not even for a second, the rationale and inevitability of moving into a breeder reactor economy.

Our minds have been constructed so, that we tend to regard as normal all the things we get used to. In the 17th century Europe people were tortured to death publicly, on market squares. People thought that this was normal, because they had seen something like this many times and were used to it. Public torture and mutilation of human beings was considered a form of free entertainment provided by the state. People working in the Nazi concentration camps during the Second World War learned to consider the things they were doing as the normal and rational thing to do.

Something similar has happened to the people working for nuclear power industries and nuclear control authorities. They are, in practice, trying to increase the number of nuclear weapons states by one hundred or so, but they have hypnotized themselves to believing that there is nothing problematic in this.

At the moment we have 30 countries that produce nuclear power, and 80 other countries which have said in the International Atomic Energy Association that they would also like to start their own, nuclear power programmes. If we have, in 2100, 110 countries with nuclear reactors, this will in practice mean 110 countries with breeder reactors, and 110 de facto nuclear weapons states, instead of the present nine.

Above all, if we move to fourth-generation nuclear reactors, every shipment or transporation of nuclear fuel to any of these reactors would always provide all the world's terrorist organizations a new opportunity of acquiring nuclear weapons.

Let's say that we would, in the future, produce 10 per cent of our energy by 1,000-megawatt breeder reactors, in a world that used three times more energy than now. To achieve this we would need something like 4,000 large breeder reactors. Let's assume that each of them received a shipment of new fuel twice a year. This would give the terrorist organizations 8,000 annual opportunities of acquiring a nuclear weapon. Eight thousand on a yearly basis. In a century this would mean 800,000 separate opportunities.

Sooner or later the worst, the unthinkable, the unimaginable, would happen.

Probability is like gravity. You can't fight gravity. The odds catch up.

At the moment only India is already constructing breeder reactors. Only one is under construction, but the final aim of the programme is to have 600 gigawatts of breeder reactors by 2060. This would, in practice, mean 1,200 Kalpakkam-sized (500 Mw) breeders or 600 somewhat larger reactors. Since most parts of India suffer from serious freshwater shortages, the breeder reactors would be cooled with sea water and thus built on coastal areas. Sodium-cooled fast breeders are especially vulnerable to tsunamis and floods, because sodium explodes when it gets in touch with air or water. One small hole or fracture in one of the coolant pipes could produce a chain of water-sodium explosions spreading simultaneously to all directions.

During the time of Mahatma Gandhi, India was the voice of reason in a world torn with imperialism, colonialism and mindless violence. Today, the Government of India seems to be leading the efforts to destroy the human race. You cannot get any farther from the teachings of the Mahatma than constructing 1,200 breeder reactors on coastal areas.

Of course, the vast majority of Indian citizens oppose these plans and will most probably ensure that such technological nightmares will never become a reality.

What To Do?

The first thing to do is to ask whether we want to have a future world in which 110 countries have nuclear weapons, and whether we want to provide (all kinds of) terrorist organizations with nuclear weapons.

If this is not what we desire, we must demand an international treaty banning the construction of nuclear reactors that use plutonium or uranium 233 or uranium

235 enriched to more than 10 per cent. There should be intergovernmental sanctions and global citizens' boycotts against the countries constructing such reactors.

We should perhaps divide nuclear reactors into five separate classes or categories, according to the risks related to nuclear weapons proliferation and to providing nuclear weapons to terrorist groups. I would propose the following classification:

Category 1: The present kind of nuclear reactors, whose fuel contains 0.7-3.6 per cent of uranium 235 (or 1.8-3.6 per cent if we exclude the CANDU-type heavy water reactors).

Category 2: MOX reactors that use a mixture of uranium and plutonium oxides, and whose fuel contains more than 4 but less than 10 per cent of various fissile isotopes (isotopes that are easy to split).

Category 3: Breeder reactors whose fuel contains, in one or several parts of the reactor, at least 10 per cent of plutonium or at least 10 per cent of plutonium and uranium 233/235.

Category 4: Breeder reactors whose fuel contains, in one or several parts of the reactor, at least 10 per cent of uranium 233 or at least 20 per cent of uranium 235, but no plutonium.

Category 5: Breder reactors whose fuel contains, in one or several parts of the reactor, almost pure uranium 233 but no plutonium.

Category 1 reactors contain fuel that cannot be used as raw material for nuclear weapons, even though they make plutonium when they begin to operate. The fuel of category 2 reactors could probably be used to make a very crude nuclear weapon, something between a dirty bomb and an actual nuclear bomb. Category 3 reactors contain fuel that can be used as such to manufacture nuclear weapons, but only by detonating the weapon with a symmetrical implosion. Category 4 reactors contain fuel that can be used to make a very simple, Hiroshima-type "pipe bomb". Category 5 reactors (including the proposed thorium reactors) contain fuel that can be used to make small but very effective nuclear weapons or triggers for two- or three-stage nuclear weapons.

In other words, category 4 and 5 reactors should be recognized to be even more dangerous than other kinds of nuclear reactors.

Free Availability of Fail-Safe Technologies

Fail-safe technologies mean systems and devices that ensure that only the president, vice-president, prime minister or in some cases another minister of the government can authorize the use of a nuclear weapon.

If we keep producing nuclear power and if new countries build their own nuclear reactors, the number of countries with nuclear weapons will keep increasing. We might soon have dozens of them, if not a hundred.

If this happens, the superpowers with the best available state-of-the-art fail-safe technology should provide their knowledge freely and free-of-charge to all new nuclear weapons states.

It would be important to ensure, that all the world's nuclear weapons are protected so well, that they cannot possibly be detonated by the classic Mad Colonel or Mad General, a military commander who loses his mind, descends into psychosis and decides to launch a nuclear war—all by himself—or by a terrorist group somehow managing to capture a nuclear weapon.

4

How Dangerous is Radioactive Pollution?

According to the official opinion of nuclear safety authorities, radioactive elements might be responsible for roughly 1 per cent of all human cancers and radioactive pollution from nuclear power plants might cause 1 per cent of this. If this opinion is correct, radioactivity would only cause about 90,000 cancers per year and radioactive pollution from nuclear power plants less than a thousand per year.

In other words, according to the currently prevailing standard scientific opinion, exposure to radioactive elements is definitely not one of our most important health problems.

However, we do not really know how dangerous different forms of radioactive pollution are.

There are three kinds of harmful radiation produced by radioactive substances: gamma rays, beta rays and alpha rays.

Gamma rays are electromagnetic radiation, just like X-rays, ultraviolet and infrared radiation, radio waves and visible light. Gamma rays, however, have a very short wavelength and contain a lot of energy. That makes them much more dangerous than the other forms of electromagnetic radiation.

Beta and alpha rays are not electromagnetic radiation but tiny, invisible particles. Beta rays are free, energetic electrons released by the decay of radioactive isotopes. Alpha rays are heavy particles that consist of neutrons and protons.

Unlike gamma rays, alpha and beta rays are not dangerous outside the body because their penetrative capacity is extremely small. They cannot even get through a thin piece of paper, not to say anything about the human skin. A couple of micrometres of anything solid or a slightly thicker layer of liquid stops them. This means that even if your skin were exposed to huge amounts of alpha and beta particles, you would not be in danger of getting radiation sickness or cancer. However, substances emitting alpha or beta rays can cause cancer and other problems if they get inside the body, if they are inhaled inside the lungs or swallowed with food or water.

Nuclear safety authorities nowadays measure radioactive exposures with a system that was developed by the Swedish scientist Rolf Maximilian Sievert.

This is why they are always speaking about millisieverts and about how many millisieverts each person has probably been exposed to.

In the Sievert scale it is assumed, that an alpha particle released inside the body is 20 times more dangerous than a similar beta particle born inside our tissues. Similarly, it is assumed that a particle striking the bladder, breasts, liver or thyroid gland is 5 times more dangerous than a particle that strikes the surface of a bone or skin. A particle hitting the lungs, pancreas or bone marrow is defined as 12 times more dangerous than a particle hitting the skin, and so on.

These figures are good guesses, or at least they used to

be good guesses when the Sievert scale was designed. However, there are two major problems with it. The first one is, that we do not know whether the numbers are correct or even roughly correct.

There have never been monstrous Nazi scientists making experiments with human subjects and exposing their internal organs to varying amounts of alpha, beta and gamma radiation to see what happens during the next twenty or thirty years.

There have been experiments with animals, but the various mammal species can have astonishingly different immunological characteristics. The worst pharmaceutical catastrophe that has ever happened, the large-scale use of the painkiller phenacetin, happened because physicians relied on experiments made with rodents. They assumed that phenacetin was not dangerous to humans because it was not dangerous to rats. For example in my own country, Finland, the use of phenacetin among a post Second World War population of three and a half million raised the annual renal mortality from three hundred to one thousand two hundred. After phenacetin was withdrawn from the pharmacies, renal mortality returned to its normal level. To my knowledge, nobody has tried to estimate the global total of victims.

The development of human cancer often takes twenty or thirty years or even more. Therefore exposing laboratory rats to large but rapid doses of radioactive substances does not tell us very much.

It is assumed that if a mouse weighs 2,000 times less than a human, a 2,000 times smaller dose of radioactivity is as dangerous to the mouse as a 2,000 times larger dose is to a human. However, this is again just a guess. It seems that a cancer can start from a single cell. What if this means that the same amount of radioactivity inhaled in the lungs is roughly as dangerous for a mouse and for a human, in terms of cancer risk, in spite of a large difference in size?

In other words, even if the Sievert scale sounds precise, it is only a collection of dozens of interlinked, educated guesses. It is closer to (science) fiction than to empirically established science fact. It would be important for the nuclear scientists and nuclear safety authorities to remember that this is the case. However, they have been using the Sievert scale for so long and got so used to it that they have almost completely forgotten that we do not really know whether all the assumptions have hit close to the mark.

Above all: in most cases we cannot really measure the radioactive exposures. But instead of admitting this openly, nuclear scientists have decided to ignore the problem.

Pretending to Measure What Cannot be Measured

Nuclear scientists and the workers of nuclear power plants assess exposures to radioactivity by dosimetres, small devices that can measure the amount of gamma radiation and certain kinds of beta radiation hitting a small transparent window on the other side of the instrument. However, the results are not given in becquerels or in how many gamma rays and/or beta rays per second there are per square centimeter, which would be the scientific and right way to define what is actually being detected. Instead, the scale of the dosimetre is in microsieverts.

This is absurd, because "microsieverts" refer to total radioactive exposure, to the sum total of external gamma, beta and alpha radiation and internal gamma, beta and alpha radiation.

As mentioned before, external exposures are much less dangerous than internal exposures, internal alpha rays are much more dangerous than gamma or beta rays, and rays hitting certain organs are more dangerous than rays hitting other organs, an internal alpha ray being 20 times more dangerous than an internal beta ray and an alpha ray hitting your lung tissue being 12 times more dangerous than an alpha ray hitting the surface of bone, and so on.

So how can you measure all this with an instrument that can, in reality, only measure external gamma and some types of beta radiation? The answer: you can't. It is like you would say that you can measure blood cholesterol by a thermometer, by just measuring the temperature of your body in degrees Celsius and dividing the number by ten to get milligrams of cholesterol per litre of blood.

In most cases the estimates of our outdoor radioactive exposures are based on measuring external gamma radiation and a part of the spectrum of the beta radiation, and on just assuming that the are no small particles that contain alpha radiators and which could be inhaled and deposited inside people's lungs.

This is not a very scientific way of measuring radioactive exposures and may explain the strange discrepancies in studies related to health effects of radiation.

Officially, the average exposure to radiation of a Finnish citizen is 5.7 millisieverts per year, of which 4 millisieverts come from the radioactive radon gas inside the apartments, 0.5 from radioactive substances in the nature, 0.7 from medical x-rays and cat scans, 0.3 from the exposure to cosmic rays and 0.4 from the radioactive substances inside the human body, meaning, above all, radioactive potassium inside our bones. This gives an impression of scientific accuracy, of something precise, of something that can be measured reliably. Unfortunately, this impression is highly misleading.

Rolf Maximilian Sievert was a scientist, and a good one. However, his followers have forgotten or almost forgotten all the uncertainties related to the Sievert scale and now take it as granted. They think that they already know roughly how many cancers different kinds of radioactive exposure can cause. So there is no need for further research, no need to ask difficult questions. If there are research reports which do not fit their predictions they will just ignore them like the US Nimbus satellite ignored the Antarctic Ozone Hole, because it was programmed to ignore impossible results.

Alice Stewart and the Survivors from Hiroshima

The Environmental Protection Agency (of the USA) admits that much - or most - of what we know about health impacts of radiation is based on studies among the survivors of Hiroshima and Nagasaki.

Hibakushas, people who survived the firestorms of Nagasaki and Hiroshima, have had a slightly—but only very slightly—higher incidence of cancer than the mainstream population of Japan. Because they were exposed to very high doses of gamma radiation, scientists have concluded that radioactivity cannot be very efficient in causing human cancer.

This line of argumentation, however, has a number of holes. One of the main criticisms was first put forward by Alice Stewart, a prominent British scientist who was the first to prove that X-rays (Röntgen rays) used in medicine can cause cancer for humans.

Most of the survivors of Hiroshima and Nagasaki got very serious second or third degree burns over much of their skin. Most people could not have survived something like this even with excellent medical care, including antibiotics to treat the horrible bacterial infections which quickly covered the wounds. The Hibakusha did not receive any antibiotics—Japan did not have them during the Second World War—and even otherwise the medical care they received was far from excellent.

According to Stewart, people who can survive such an ordeal are kind of immunological superhumans, the immunological elite of an elite. The immunological elite of an elite should have a much lower than average rate of cancer, because we get cancer when our immunological defence systems fail. If the elite of an elite has, contrary to the basic prediction, a slightly higher than average rate of cancer, due to their exposure to gamma rays, this does not prove that radioactive exposures are relatively harmless!

If the survivors had 1 per cent higher than the average rate of cancer, their cancer risk had in reality increased a lot and possibly multiplied, instead of increasing only by 1 per cent.

I have always found Alice Stewart's point convincing, and nobody has ever been able to present good arguments against it. I am inclined to think that Stewart may have been right in this issue, as well. History may repeat itself, here: the majority of the mainstream scientists also opposed —fiercely, aggressively and for a remarkably long time— Stewart's studies about the cancer risks related to X-rays.

Another methodological problem related to Hiroshima

and Nagasaki us that even though hibaskushas were exposed to high doses of gamma radiation, they did not necessarily inhale large amounts of radioactive particles in their lungs.

The blasts devastated a much smaller area than the ensuing firestorms. All the people inside the fire perimeter died. There were no survivors in this area.

The heat of the explosion raised most of the radioactive dust into great heights. The firestorm strengthened these rising air currents and produced hurricane-strength winds blowing from the perimeter towards the firestorm.

This means that most radioactive particles may have risen up and then dropped down, typically much farther, over different parts of Japan. In other words: also the control group—other Japanese people—were exposed to radioactive small and nano particles and inhaled them into their lungs. We cannot even say, with any certainty, whether the people in the surrounding areas got more or less radioactive particulate matter inside their lungs than hibakushas. During the next eighteen years all the people in Japan—and people everywhere on the planet—were then exposed to radioactive substances from nuclear weapon tests.

A Fully Blind Study: The New Research Innovation by Nuclear Scientists

Small particles floating in the air are, without doubt, the most dangerous form of radioactive pollution. They are light enough to be inhaled, but they do not necessarily come out of the lungs when the air is exhaled. They can remain in alveoli, tiny gas-exchanging chambers inside the lungs, or concentrate in the bifurcation points of bronchioles, the lungs' tiny air tubes. They can also move from lungs to other internal organs or get stuck in bacterial plaques in the walls of our arteries.

In other words, this kind of tiny radioactive particles can remain inside the human body for years or decades. Because of this, they may be very efficient in causing cancer. According to present scientific understanding, we get cancer when the same DNA strands are damaged repeatedly and the problem finally gets out of control. If this is correct, it is hard to imagine a more efficient cancer-causing mechanism than tiny radioactive particles permanently lodged inside our most vulnerable tissues.

However, it is extremely difficult to measure the exact scale of the danger.

Epidemiologists nowadays think that only the so-called double blind studies can give reliable information on whether a certain factor can cause a certain disease with a certain probability, or whether a certain medicine has a genuine impact on a disease it is supposed to cure or at least alleviate.

The blind method was originally invented by the British chemist, science fiction writer and poet Humphry Davy during the late 1800s. Davy was trying to find out whether nitrous oxide could have any beneficial uses in medicine. He started by simply asking people to describe how the gas influenced them, whether it eased their symptoms and so on. Davy soon noticed that people's accounts were utterly unreliable. People seemed to adjust their assessment on the impact of nitrous oxide gas depending on what they wanted to believe, on how they wanted the gas to affect them, or on what they thought Davy wanted to hear.

Davy solved the problem by dividing his human guinea

pigs into two categories. The other group was given nitrous oxide and the other group was only given plain air. The people did not themselves know whether they got air or nitrous oxide. Everyone thought that they were given the real thing.

Davy's method has since then become the standard method of empirical medicine. The present state-of-the-art is called the double-blind study. In double-blind studies even the researchers themselves do not know who is getting the real drug and who is getting placebo, until the data has been analysed.

But... how can you do a double blind study on the impact of radioactive particles inhaled in human lungs?

The main problem is that there is no way of measuring how much radioactivity in the form of small particles a person has inhaled inside his body, during his lifetime. We can, of course, measure the amount of uranium in a person's urine, but this only tells us roughly how much uranium dust the person has inhaled or swallowed during the preceding 24 hours or so. There is no way to measure, for example, annual or lifetime exposures and to compare them with the cancer mortality of different groups of people. We cannot act like the Nazis would have done in Auschwitz: we cannot expose some people to radioactive substances and others to a harmless placebo.

Because of this it has turned out to be very difficult to assess, accurately, how many cancers, for example, nuclear accidents and the uranium dust produced by depleted uranium shells have produced.

Nuclear powers detonated 423 nuclear weapons in the atmosphere between 1945 and 1980. The combined total explosive power of these nuclear bombs has been estimated at 545 megatons, equivalent to 44,000 Hiroshimas. However, it has been extremely difficult to assess how many cancers these 423 radioactive fallouts have caused.

Everybody was exposed, so there are no control groups. Everybody inhaled radioactive particles from the nuclear detonations and all of us have incorporated radioactive tritium from nuclear explosions and nuclear power plants inside our DNA strands, but different individuals have probably wildly different lifetime exposures. How can we calculate the danger when there is no way of measuring the exposure of each individual?

The problems in assessing the health impact of the nuclear fallout from Chernobyl constitute another clear demonstration of the problem.

Counted in curies, the accident in Chernobyl spread about 0.5 per cent of the radioactivity inside one nuclear reactor (50 million curies, according to the International Atomic Energy Association) into the atmosphere. The accident released most of the radioactive substances that are easily vaporized, but only a tiny part of the uranium and plutonium was spread over the northern hemisphere as small and nanoparticles.

An official study made in the West by the International Atomic Energy Association and the World Health Organization estimated, that radioactive exposures caused by the accident in Chernobyl might finally result in 4,000 extra cancer deaths. On the other hand, Russian, Belorussian and Ukrainian physicians and scientists have published at least 730 scientific studies according to which the accident has already led to notable increases in many types of cancers and numerous other illnesses in the affected areas. The picture that emerges from these seven hundred plus studies is dramatically different than the official view promoted by the UN organizations, Western governments and nuclear industries. If these seven hundred studies are closer to the mark, the final death toll of the Chernobyl accident will be counted in hundreds of thousands, if not millions. For the public, such a discrepancy in predictions, amounting to three full orders of magnitude, has of course been more than slightly confusing.

This far Western scientists have simply ignored the Russian, Ukrainian and Belorussian studies as "nonsense", which has been arrogant and more than somewhat unfair. There could be differences in the methodologies used in each country, but Russian, Ukrainian and Belorussian scientists certainly understand the basic issues and problems of epidemiology, and they have—in most cases—carefully described the methods they had used in their studies.

The nuclear establishment has also ignored all the Western studies that have produced "impossible" results. In many countries there was a clear peak in infant mortality during the three years following Chernobyl. For instance, in Britain there were 2,000 extra infant deaths during these years. Similar peaks in infant mortality were reported from Turkey, Poland and some parts of Germany. Moreover, the decline in the percentage of observed pregnancies ending in still birth went flat after Chernobyl in many countries. After a few years the curve again started to fall down.

Spring westerlies carried a part of Chernobyl's fallout to India, which is almost never mentioned. Indian physicians reported that while infant mortality in India had been dropping with a rate of three per cent per year before Chernobyl, it only fell by 1.1 per cent per year during the years 1986-88, after which the annual reduction again rose to three per cent. Such a statistical anomaly was equivalent to one million extra infant deaths. This can, of course, be a coincidence. A correlation does not yet prove that there is a cause-and-effect relation between two things, it only implies that something like this might exist.

To my knowledge, the figures mentioned above have not been disputed, because they are based in official demographic statistics, but a causal connection with Chernobyl has been vehemently denied by the mainstream opinion.

The main opposing argument has been, that further studies, for example, in Germany did not find a correlation between increased infant mortality and a high level of radioactive pollution from Chernobyl. In other words: there were no additional infant deaths in Germany's most badly polluted areas, compared with regions that received less radioactivity from Chernobyl. Case closed.

Except it was the areas, where it rained when the radioactive cloud was passing over them which received the highest amount of fallout. In these areas radioactive particles came down inside rain drops. Most radioactive substances are not very dangerous when swallowed with food or water, because they mostly come out from the body after a few hours or days, only. As I have already mentioned, the most dangerous form of radioactive pollution are small hot particles that are so light that they are easily inhaled inside the lungs, but so heavy that they do not easily get out from the alveoli with the return flow of air. If such hot particles park themselves inside the alveols and then move to other internal organs, they can remain inside the body for years or decades, instead of only hours or days. The difference is very important, because there are

8,784 hours in a year with 366 days.

What if many of the areas that "were not badly polluted" received less radioactivity, but in a more dangerous form? When radioactive particles fall down with rain, they cannot be inhaled. Therefore a small amount of "dry" pollution could, in effect, be thousands if not tens of thousands of times more dangerous than an equivalent amount of radioactivity inside falling raindrops.

In other words: all the "carefully done" Western control studies about the consequences of Chernobyl may have been worthless, or worse than worthless. In reality the scientists did not have a clue of what was compared with what.

This means, in practice, that Western scientists with their obsession about the elegant double-blind method have actually—in this case—used a new kind of method that could be called the triple-blind or fully blind method.

They have their control groups, but in reality they cannot have any idea of who has been exposed to what. There is no way to know whether the "exposed group" has in reality inhaled a larger or smaller amount of radioactive aerosols in their lungs than the "control group". When this cannot be measured or estimated in a reliable way—and it cannot —it is not possible to conduct a proper double-blind study. If you still try to do it, the whole exercise becomes counter-productive, because it produces an illusion of scientific accuracy in a situation where precise measurements cannot be made.

For this reason, the Russian, Belorussian and Ukrainian studies which have used a somewhat cruder methodology and just followed whether the incidence and prevalence of certain diseases is increasing or decreasing might actually be more reliable and informative than the Western, quasi-elegant fully blind studies.

Is there a way to break the deadlock and move forward?

Actually, there might be. There is one form of aerosol-formed radioactive exposure, which can be measured relatively accurately, so that we can estimate roughly how much radioactivity each exposed person has inhaled in his lungs, in the form of highly radioactive small and nanoparticles.

This form of radioactive exposure is called smoking.

How does Tobacco Cause Cancer?

When I visited India for the first time, in 1984, I was shocked by the amount of smoke poor women were daily exposed to, when they were cooking with wood or cow dung inside their houses, in houses that had no chimneys.

I was also somewhat puzzled, because I understood that poor women must have been doing the same for thousands of years.

I had just read that lung cancer used to be a very rare disease in Europe before the Second World War. In the Britain of the 1930s, old doctors and even medical professors thronged to watch the obductions of people who had died of lung cancer, because most of them had never seen a case, before.

According to standard scientific wisdom lung cancer and other tobacco-related cancers are caused by the numerous carcinogenic chemicals present in tobacco smoke. I started to wonder how this could be.

Women in 170 million households using traditional cooking stoves and solid fuels were daily exposing themselves to huge amounts of woodfuel smoke in India, equivalent to smoking at least 20 packs of cigarettes a day.

According to studies summarized in the State of India's Environment 1984-85 report the particulate matter concentrations in the air of Indian kitchens sometimes reached 56 600 micrograms per cubic metre, 2,240 times more than the World Health Organization recommendation of 25 micrograms. The women who did the cooking in Ahmedabad inhaled 6,100 micrograms of benzo(a)pyrene in a year, while the proposed international recommendation was only 3.5 micrograms or almost two thousand times less. Gujarati women cooking the food annually inhaled 21,000 micrograms of suspended particulates from fuelwood. They annually inhaled a dose of small particles—containing all kinds of chemical carcinogens—a hundred times larger than the maximum level recommended by the World Health Organization and hundreds of larger than the people's average annual exposure in many European countries.

Even in Europe and North America electricity and natural gas are relatively recent inventions. Besides, people in all continents have been smoking tobacco, marihuana and opium for centuries. Indians have been consuming huge amounts of tiny, filterless cigarettes known as bidis for a very long time.

In China smoking was very common already during the Ming dynasty. According to a contemporary report, in the southwest of the country almost all people, whether old or young, could not stop themselves from smoking from morning till night. The writer Wang Pu wrote in the 1600s that "all the people, even boys not four feet tall, were smoking". During the Qing dynasty men boasted that they were unable to eat, converse or think unless they kept smoking. Lu Yao's Smoking Manual (Yan pu) from the year

1774 recommended people to smoke when waking up, after the meal, with guests, while writing, when growing tired from reading and while waiting for a good friend. In the 19th century there was, both in Europe and in China, a huge number of people who chain-smoked from the morning till late evening.

Taking all this into consideration, how is it possible, that lung cancer only became a common disease after the Second World War?

In England and Wales about 250 people died of lung cancer in 1920. In 1960 the figure was 10 000, forty times more. People living in Britain in the late 1800s and early 1900s had definitely been exposed to much larger amounts of woodfuel and coal smoke than the smokers of post-Second World War Britain. Their air had been much more polluted because most of the people had been cooking with woodfuel or coal instead of gas and electricity.

I felt that something was missing from the picture, but I forgot the problem for a long time because of other urgent work. I returned to the issue only in 2003, when I realized that it might be interesting to study whether there are significant amounts of radioactive substances in tobacco. Tobacco was, after all, a very greedy plant, devouring huge amounts of nutrients from the soil. What if it also collected radioactive substances from the ground? Radioactive particles from nuclear detonations, Sellafield and Chernobyl, uranium dust from coal- and peat-fired power plants and so on.

I quickly found out, that there was some radioactive polonium 210 in tobacco smoke, so the hypothesis started to look genuinely interesting. I even based a whole novel (a thriller), called *Litium 6* (Lithium 6 in Finnish) on the idea.

Only slightly later did I find out that there was nothing original in my idea, because it had already been published forty years earlier. The only new aspect in my stream of thinking was that I had arrived at the same conclusions via a different route, by wondering why the massive exposures of Indian women to woodfuel smoke had caused so few lung cancers.

Linda R. Hunt had proved, already in 1964, that tobacco leaves were much more radioactive than tobacco ash, and that the difference was mostly caused by radioactive polonium 210 that did not stay in the ash but was inhaled into a smoker's lungs with tobacco smoke. Most of the polonium in tobacco had been produced by the decay of uranium atoms, which had been spread on the fields as an impurity or contaminant of phosphate fertilizers.

Further studies showed, that the radioactive polonium in tobacco smoke tended to stick to the bifurcation points of bronchioles, the tiny air tubes inside lungs, and create radioactive hot spots in these junctions.

I learned that in the late 1960s physicians had actually believed, that most tobacco-related cancers were caused by radioactive polonium. Then other researchers had shown, that it was also possible to cause cancer to laboratory animals with certain chemical carcinogens that existed in tobacco smoke. The polonium theory was suddenly swept under the carpet as if it had never existed. From then on, the official assumption was that only something like 0.1 or 0.05 per cent of all tobacco-related cancers were caused by radioactive elements, if even that, and that 99.9 or 99.95 per cent were caused by chemical carcinogens like nitrosamines.

But many things actually support the polonium theory,

including the following facts:

- it is very difficult to cause lung cancer for laboratory animals with tobacco smoke that does not contain any radioactive polonium 210
- it was very easy to cause a lung cancer for 94 per cent of the laboratory animals by making them inhale polonium 210 aerosols, and even the tiniest amounts of polonium caused lung cancer to 10-36 per cent of the animals
- when filters were added to cigarettes they reduced the amount of the most important chemical carcinogens (like nitrosamines) in tobacco smoke by 80 per cent (to one-fifth), while the amount of polonium in tobacco increased three- to sixfold and tobacco's ability to cause cancer increased two- or three-fold
- lung cancer was not common before the Second World War, in spite of the fact that people were smoking and were also exposed to huge amounts of smoke from fuelwood, crop residues and cowdung used as fuel, and from nitrosamines produced by smoking, fire-curing and deep-frying food

For these reasons some serious epidemiologists, including the former US Surgeon General Everet C. Koop have said, that up to 90 per cent of all tobacco-related cancers might be caused by radioactive polonium in tobacco smoke.

What, Then, are the Counter-Arguments?

In a way, there is only one, which goes roughly as follows: "Because we know that radioactive exposures are not very dangerous, the amount of radioactivity in tobacco smoke is far too small to be responsible for a significant faction of tobacco-related cancers. Therefore radioactive polonium in tobacco can only cause very few cases of cancer."

It is true, that the amount of radioactive polonium in cigarettes is tiny. Between half a billion and one billion polonium 210 atoms decay in the average smoker's lungs during one year. This is a very small amount of radioactivity! However, the decay of polonium 210 produces a heavy alpha particle, and the radioactive hot spots in the lungs keep bombarding the same vulnerable cells over and over again. What if even this amount of alpha bombardment inside the lungs or pancreas is a major cancer risk?

I would say that the case against polonium is not very convincing and that the arguments for polonium being the main cancer-causing agent in tobacco smoke are much stronger. Why has polonium been swept under the carpet?

The timing may reveal something for us. In 1973 OPEC was able to quadruple the price of crude oil. The move caused a recession and widespread panic in the West. Western governments started to invest heavily in new energy technologies that reduced their dependency of oil. Nuclear power was seen as the key answer to the energy crises and to the threat of deepening dependency on oil-exporting Arab countries. It may be that in this atmosphere the governments were reluctant to "scare the people unnecessarily" by informing them about the dangers of radioactive substances. If the people had thought that tobacco-related cancers were largely caused by radioactivity, they would have been more afraid of radioactive substances and of nuclear power.

Besides, the USA, Soviet Union, Britain, France and China had exploded 423 nuclear weapons and exposed every human being on the planet to significant quantities of radioactive substances. What if this would finally cause tens or even hundreds of millions of cancers all over the world?

If a major part of tobacco-related cancers are caused by radioactive polonium 210, also the radioactive fallout from nuclear detonations in the atmosphere must have caused many cancers. If polonium is accepted as the main cause of lung cancer, the fallout from nuclear weapons trials would be seen as a possible, if not the proven, cause to every single cancer on the planet.

As a main rule, I do not believe in conspiracy theories, but there is something very odd in the way the polonium hypothesis was suddenly buried in the middle of the 1970s.

The issue is still very relevant, because tobacco now causes between one-fifth and one-third of all cancers, and up to one half of all cancer deaths.

Lung cancer currently kills about 1.6 million people in a year. This has been predicted to rise to 3 million in 2030 and might well rise further to 4 or 5 million by 2050. We know for sure that tobacco causes at least 70 and possibly more than 90 per cent of all lung cancers. Besides this it is almost certain that smoking is also responsible for a substantial percentage of the cancers of pancreas, lips, mouth, throat, stomach, larynx, bladder and gullet, even though physicians have been forced to be careful when saying anything about this, because of the aggressive resistance strategies of the Big Tobacco.

Tobacco-related cancers are more lethal than most other tumours. Eighty per cent of the women who get breast cancer, 95 of the men who get prostate cancer and 99.5 of the people who get a non-melanoma skin cancer are still alive after 5 years, but only 14 per cent of the people who get lung cancer, only a few per cent of those who get pancreatic cancer and only 50 per cent of the people who get a cancer of the throat.

Cancer now kills nine million people, every year, and this is likely to increase to twenty million by 2030. The final peak of the cancer epidemic could be even higher. In the West almost one half of all people now get cancer during their lifetime. It would be of crucial importance for us to know, whether a much higher percentage of all cancers than we have thought are caused by polonium 210 and other radioactive substances.

Luckily, there is a way to find out what is the truth about the matter. We should ban the sales of tobacco containing significant amounts of polonium.

This would, in any case, save numerous lives. If the mainstream opinion of Western nuclear scientists is correct, the move will only save a few thousand lives in a year, globally, a few hundred thousand people per century. But even this would be important. Human lives should be sacred, every life should count.

On the other hand, if it turns out that polonium 210 has been responsible for 20, 30, 50 or even 90 per cent of all tobacco-related cancers, the move might save millions or lives, every year, hundreds of millions or a billion during the next one hundred years.

According to studies conducted by the US tobacco industry and made public via the order of the High Court most of the polonium could easily be removed from the phosphate fertilizers and 25 per cent by washing the tobacco plants. Of the rest, 92 per cent could be removed from tobacco smoke by adding ion-exchange filters to cigarettes. Natural farming of tobacco without any phosphate fertilizers might produce even better results.

Due to the initiative of the Finnish non-governmental organization CED (Coalition for Environment and Development) Satu Hassi and Carl Schlyter, two Green members of the European Parliament proposed in March 2013 that the European Union should restrict the maximum allowable amount of polonium 210 in tobacco to 0.002 picocuries per cigarette, one-twentieth of the present average. This would still have been technically easy and the cost of such a 95 per cent reduction in tobacco's polonium content would have been very low.

When the proposal was discussed in the committee for Environment, health and food safety of the European parliament, the principle that the maximum amount of plutonium cigarettes can contain should be restricted—the recital calling for a low threshold for polonium in cigarettes—was accepted by 39 votes for and 31 against. Also the amendment calling for the development of a standard measuring technique (a so-called ISO standard) for tobacco in polonium was accepted by a narrow margin (35-34).

The proposal about actually restricting the amount of polonium in tobacco to 0.002 picocuries per cigarette already in 2013 was defeated by a strong lobby by tobacco and nuclear industries and by a coalition of MEPs (members of the European parliament) supportive to their causes. The vote was even, 35-35, but in a draw the original proposal by the European Commission wins and the proposal for an amendment to the directive loses.

The results remained the same also in the final votes on October 8, 2013, in the plenary of the European parliament, but in a later meeting of the EU member states even the principal decision about limiting the amount of polonium in cigarettes some day in the future was left out from the directive. In other words, the European Union decided that it will not do anything to reduce the amount of an important carcinogen in tobacco, even though this would have prevented a large number of cancer deaths with a negligible financial cost.

Why did EU make such a decision?

There is a strong pro-nuclear group in the European parliament. The pro-nuclear MEPs of course understand that radioactivity in tobacco has nothing or very little to do with the production of nuclear power. However, they tend to oppose, more or less automatically, anything that might reduce the popularity or profitability of nuclear power.

If coal power kills 100,000 people in a year and nuclear power only 1,000 it is easy to argue that nuclear power is a better alternative, from a public health view-point, in spite of the fact that coal-fired thermal power plants produce many times more energy than nuclear facilities. However, if it turned out that radioactive polonium in tobacco smoke is for example fifty times more dangerous than we have thought, also the radioactive exposures related to nuclear power plants, nuclear accidents, nuclear fuel reprocessing plants and uranium mines might cause dozens of times more cancer than has been assumed. If this were the case, and a relatively small amount of nuclear power would be responsible for, let's say, 50,000 cancer deaths per year instead of only 1,000 it would no longer be possible to claim that nuclear energy is less dangerous for people's health than coal power.

Tobacco industry, on the other hand, fears that people would begin to link smoking with radioactivity. They know that they lose customers whenever a smoker dies of lung cancer, but for them widespread alarm about radioactive substances in tobacco were even worse.

Radioactivity is psychologically a much more frightening thing than smoke, because smoke is a very common and ordinary thing. It is part of our everyday lives, we have all seen smoke countless times and are so used to it that we cannot really fear it—emotionally—even when we know, rationally, that smoke can be dangerous for our health.

If people started thinking that tobacco causes cancer through radioactive exposures, many more people would probably quit smoking. The idea of radioactivity would make smoking feel more dangerous, even though most of the tobacco-related deaths are caused by emphysema and cardiovascular disease, which have nothing to do with radioactivity.

The Mystery of Cancer

A study that investigated the rate of cancer among ancient Egyptian mummies produced an astonishing result: only one mummy in almost one thousand had cancerous tumours, even though mummification should have preserved the tumours.

Lets imagine, as a thought experiment, that all medical treatment of cancer in Europe would suddenly stopped for a decade and that all the people dying in Europe were mummified, Egyptian style. How many of them would have tumours that could be discovered by future researchers? At least five hundred in a thousand, and possibly more.

For example, in Finland, more than one half of all people now get at least one cancer during their life. The rate is still increasing and these are only the cancers that are diagnosed.

When an old person dies of a stroke, heart attack or pneumonia, there are no autopsies and nobody checks whether the deceased also had a cancer. It is almost certain that many of the people now dying in Europe for other reasons also have a cancer during the time of their death, even though it was never found by the physicians. This means that the real figure might be even six or seven hundred per one thousand.

In other words: the incidence of cancer has increased by a factor of five hundred and possibly by a factor of six or seven hundred, compared with ancient Egypt.

Part of the change can be explained by people's increased longevity. We have more cancer because we live longer and are not killed by infectious diseases as often as before. This is indisputable: 89 per cent of all cancers are diagnosed in people that are over 50 years of age and 90 per cent of the ancient people whose remains we have been able to study have died before their 55th birthday.

However, many of the people who were mummified in Egypt were rather old when they died, with hardened arteries and brittle, osteoporotic bones.

And even if we assumed that 90 per cent were younger than 55 when they died, we still had five or ten times less cancer than we should have. This is very odd, because our exposure to most cancer-causing factors has been greatly diminished.

This point may come as a surprise, but we know that some viruses and bacteria—many of which are sexually transmitted diseases—cause or at least trigger a significant percentage of all cancers. Most stomach cancers are caused by helicobacter pylori, which can be treated by antibiotics. Cervical cancers are caused or triggered by chlamydia infections and human papilloma viruses (HPVs). HPVs probably cause a number of other cancers, as well, including the cancer of the prostate in men. Liver cancers are caused by hepatitis B (and possibly hepatitis C) and it is almost certain that the mouse breast tumour virus (MBTV) has been responsible for a significant percentage of all human breast cancers.

Our exposure to different viral and bacterial infections is now much less than it used to be. We can prevent hepatitis and HPV infections by vaccinations and chlamydia and helicobacter infections can be cured with antibiotics. Sex workers and most other people practising casual sex nowadays use condoms, which effectively prevent infections that can be transmitted via a sexual intercourse. Modern condoms were only developed in the 1930s. Because of the improvements in housing conditions and because half of the world's population now live in cities, our exposure to MBTV has been much reduced.

Some pesticides still in use may cause cancer, but as a general rule it must be said that our overall exposure to strong chemical carcinogens via our food, water and air must have diminished, dramatically, after the Second World War.

As mentioned above, women cooking with firewood inside houses that have no chimneys expose themselves to vastly higher concentrations of numerous chemical carcinogens than smokers, not to say anything about non-smoking Europeans or North Americans. As mentioned before, this kind of exposures have been there for millennia and they also existed in ancient Egypt.

The food of present-day Europeans and North Americans contains a much smaller amount of chemical carcinogens than it used to contain. Smoked and fire-cured foods and foods deep-fried in hot oil often contain very large concentrations of nitrosamines and other carcinogens. Most of our food used to be made with these methods, but this is no longer the case. Many of the bacteria and fungi that can infest our food also produce carcinogens, but this problem should be smaller than during the previous centuries. Our exposure to asbestos reached its peak during the Second World War, and has diminished since then.

Most cancer researchers now agree that both chronic inflammation and major immunological storms caused by influenza or other major infections increase our risk of getting cancer. Malaria and intestinal parasites probably increase our cancer risk by forcing the immune system to suppress its own activity so that its attacks against the parasites will not cause lethal damage to the body. Major bone fractures also seem to be a risk factor, especially if they do not heal properly. All these problems are nowadays less common than they used to be.

We know that vitamin D deficiency is an important risk factor of cancer but even this problem has probably been more significant, before. Ricketts, the most extreme symptom of serious vitamin D deficiency, used to be extremely common in Europe and North America but has since then almost disappeared.

So how can we have five hundred times more cancer than before? And why did the incidence of some cancers, like lung cancer, explode during the 20th century? Why did the incidence of lung cancer increase 40-fold in England and Wales in a few decades?

Besides the increased longevity, there are only two other cancer-causing factors that have definitely become more prominent during the modern times: many of us have been forced to adopt unnatural daily rhythms and most of us are exposed to much higher amounts of gamma, alpha and beta radiation than the people who lived before the 20th century. All life on earth has adjusted to 24-hour-rhythms, and according to recent studies such 24-hour or circadian rhythms greatly influence almost everything that happens in our bodies. Messing with the circadian rhythms seems to be a major cancer risk. I come back to this in the last chapter.

But there are also approximately fifteen different mechanisms which have greatly increased our annual radiation doses.

Tobacco smoke now contains significant quantities of polonium 210 and everybody has been exposed to tobacco smoke, not only the smokers. The burning of other biomass produced on fields which have received uranium as a contaminant of phosphate fertilizers may cause similar problems, although on a much smaller scale. Some of our cancers may come from polonium and other radioactive substances in our food and water.

We have been burning huge and growing amounts of coal in factories and thermal power stations. Coal always contains small amounts of uranium. A large coal-fired power station typically spreads about five tons of uranium per year in the atmosphere, in the form of small and nanoparticles that can be inhaled inside the lungs or that can rain down on fields growing food for human consumption. When the uranium atoms decay they again produce polonium, radium, radon and other dangerous radioactive substances. Peat-burning power stations produce even higher radioactive emissions than coal-fired plants.

Nuclear power plants and nuclear fuel reprocessing facilities routinely release significant amounts of tritium and other radioactive substances into our environment. Nuclear accidents have released large amounts of radioactivity and during 1945-63 the nuclear weapons tests did the same. The tens of millions of depleted uranium shells fired by the US military in Iraq, Kosovo and Bosnia have polluted large areas with fine uranium dust, because depleted uranium shells burn to a mildly radioactive aerosol when they hit a hard target.

Uranium mining produces mildly radioactive dust, polonium, radon and radium, as well as the asphalt ground to dust under car tires. Living in a concrete building exposes us to radon, polonium and radium because the sand in concrete always contains varying concentrations of uranium. The number of people living and working in concrete apartment houses instead of houses constructed of wood and mud has multiplied after the Second World War. The construction of very air-tight houses can make the problem worse. Swedish researchers have shown, that this can increase the people's exposure to radon released from the concrete structures by a factor of three.

Flying high in the atmosphere with jet planes exposes us to gamma radiation in the form cosmic rays. Air hostesses have a several times higher risk of breast cancer than other women.

What if a majority of all human cancers are caused by these radioactive exposures? As said before, it is difficult to find out, whether this is so, because it is impossible to measure people's lifetime exposures to radioactive substances via food, water and air.

The only realistic and feasible way to clarify the truth

about this matter may be to enact legislation, that restricts the maximum amount of plutonium that cigarettes can contain for example to five per cent of the present level.

If this does not reduce the number of tobacco-related cancers occurring after twenty or thirty years, the estimates of national nuclear safety authorities have probably been relatively accurate, and radioactive exposures are only responsible for roughly one per cent of all human cancer. On the other hand, if the removal of polonium from cigarettes reduces tobacco-related cancer mortality by for instance 90 per cent, we should conclude, that also the other radioactive exposures may be much more dangerous than we have thought.

It may be very difficult to restrict tobacco's polonium content as long as we keep producing nuclear power as long as there are strong pro-nuclear lobbies in the various parliaments, opposing everything that has something to do with protecting people from radioactive exposures.

Pro-tobacco and pro-nuclear lobbies are, together, a far too formidable coalition.

However, if the nuclear industry dies out because of the economic and competitive challenges posed by solar, wind, biomass and geothermal energy, also the pro-nuclear lobbies inside the parliaments vanish. At that time it becomes, for the first time in history, possible to find out whether the majority of all human cancers are actually caused by radioactive exposures.

Tritiated Earth?

When everything goes well, nuclear power reactors only produce two kinds of routine radioactive emissions: radioactive noble gases (like xenon 137, xenon 135, krypton

90 and krypton 85) and tritium, the radioactive isotope of hydrogen (hydrogen 3).

Xenon and krypton as such are not likely to be very dangerous. However, it should not be forgotten that xenon 137 decays to cesium 137 and krypton 90 to strontium 90, both of which are considered extremely lethal, even by nuclear scientists.

Tritium deserves even more attention, because it can replace ordinary hydrogen in the bases – adenine, thymine, guanine and cytosine - of which our DNA molecules and thus our genes consist of. Adenine, cytocine and guanine contain five hydrogen atoms and thymine contains six of them. If some of these hydrogen atoms are replaced by tritium inside the cells of a human embryo, foetus or child, the beta radiation may seriously damage the DNA and cause stillbirths and cancer. Tritium has a half-life of 12.3 years and is thus roughly five hundred million times more radioactive than uranium 238.

Unfortunately nobody knows exactly how dangerous tritium is for the unborn and small children. Some nuclear power complexes and nuclear fuel reprocessing facilities have traditionally released their tritium into the sea, where it is diluted with ordinary seawater. The British nuclear reprocessing plant in Sellafield made the whole Sea of Ireland so polluted with tritium, that the Irish people collected a petition against Sellafield, signed by more than one million people.

Most nuclear power plants use another method. They have high chimneys, and ventilate tritium and the other radioactive gases out of them to great heights, thus spreading them over a very large area. In most cases tritium is burned to tritiated water before it is released into the atmosphere. If you have ever wondered why nuclear power plants need chimneys, this is the answer to your question.

Unfortunately the habit of spreading the tritium over a much wider area does not make it less dangerous, it only makes it much more difficult to find out exactly how many cancers, still births and other problems are caused by it. If the tritium is released into the air at a height of two metres or so, it would be easy to measure its health impact simply by checking whether there are any extra childhood cancers in the nearby areas. But when tritium is channelled into great heights, only a very small part of it drops down almost immediately as tritiated rainwater, and the rest can be transported hundreds or even thousands of kilometres further.

In Germany children living close to nuclear power plants have a 22 per cent higher risk of cancer than other children. Infants and very small children have a 54 per cent higher than normal cancer risk, and their risk of getting leukemia is 76 per cent above the average. This difference may or may not be caused by the small percentage of tritium that falls down as rainwater already in the nearby areas. Within five kilometres of nuclear power plants the additional risks for small children were even larger: 117 per cent for leukemia and 60 per cent for solid cancers.

In India a study conducted by Sampoorna Kranti Vidyalaya (SKV) found that the villages close to the Rajasthan Atomic Power Station had an extremely high rate of tumours, stillbirths, neonatal deaths, spontaneous abortions and stillbirths. This was remarkable, because the people in these neighbouring villages were considerably wealthier than the inhabitants of an average village in rural Rajasthan, thanks to employment opportunities provided by the nuclear facility.

Reactor design has a huge impact on the size of tritium emissions. In Finland the two 220 Mw nuclear reactors in Loviisa annually release into the environment roughly 500 curies (17 terabecquerels) of tritium, while the two considerably larger reactors in Olkiluoto only release about 70 curies (2.4 terabecquerels) per year. However, the nuclear company Teollisuuden Voima has applied and got a permission for releasing almost 6,000 curies or 200 terabecquerels of tritium per year from its new EPR nuclear power reactor, eighty times more than the present combined annual emissions from Olkiluoto. As I am writing this it is still impossible to say whether this level of emissions will be realized also in practice, because Olkiluoto 3 is still under construction.

Some relatively small nuclear reactors in India have even higher tritium emissions, up to 100,000 curies (!) per year and the nuclear fuel reprocessing plants also produce huge amounts of tritium. If much of our electricity would, in the future, come from fourth-generation nuclear power plants the nuclear fuel reprocessing facilities that manufactured their fuel might annually produce millions or tens of millions of curies of tritium.

We should get a better idea on the health risks of tritium before we start moving towards such a Tritiated Earth scenario.

5

How Much Radiation Could a Nuclear Accident Release?

As mentioned before, the nuclear accident in Chernobyl released between 50 and 140 million curies or 2-5 terabecquerels of radioactivity. For instance in Finland nuclear safety authorities have been saying that this was about the worst conceivable radioactive release from a nuclear power plant that could ever happen.

According to the Finnish Nuclear Safety Centre even in the worst possible scenario only the easily vaporizable elements like Cesium 137 and radioactive gases like argon and xenon can be released into the atmosphere in the form of radioactive aerosol. This is what happened in Chernobyl.

But can we be certain that Chernobyl was the worst-case-scenario?

A large nuclear reactor typically contains 100-150 tons of nuclear fuel. When nuclear fuel goes inside a reactor it produces about 0.3 curies of radioactivity per tonne. However, while the reactor is operating, nuclear fuel is continuously bombarded by neutrons that transform parts of the nuclear fuel and its cladding or protective cover to new isotopes, most of which are highly radioactive. Because of these radioactive impurities, induced or artificial radioactivity, each ton of nuclear fuel contains approximately 300 million curies of radioactivity when it has to be changed and taken out of the reactor.

This means that the amount of radioactivity in nuclear fuel has increased approximately one billion times and that the whole reactor now contains tens of billions of curies of it. The radioactive impurities in nuclear fuel are extremely dangerous if they are released into the environment, especially if they are released in the form of aerosol, small and nanoparticles floating in the air.

The decay of all these radioactive substances also produces a lot of heat. Nuclear reactors have been programmed to shut down automatically if something goes wrong. However, the decay of the radioactive impurities that have been accumulating in the nuclear fuel cannot be shut down but keeps producing significant amounts of heat for decades, even after the reactor has been stopped. In nuclear power plants the production of massive amounts of such residual heat is the worst danger in emergency situations.

The actual nuclear fuel of most present nuclear power plants is uranium oxide that contains 1.8-3.6. per cent of the isotope uranium 235. Some reactors use a mixture of uranium and plutonium oxides, or MOX (mixed oxides) fuel. Uranium and plutonium have been burned to oxides so they cannot ignite and burn.

However, the uranium or plutonium fuel actually exists in the form of small tablets inside the so-called zirconium cladding, an alloy of zirconium and other elements. It could be said that nuclear fuel rods actually mainly consist of a zirconium alloy that also contains uranium tablets. This is a potential problem, because unlike the uranium and plutonium oxides, the zirconium cladding—making most of the mass of the fuel rods—can burn. If the containment structures of a nuclear reactor are ruptured by steam or hydrogen explosions or by tiny nuclear explosions (like in Chernobyl) or if part of the fuel rods melt and burn a hole into the containment shield so that fuel rods are exposed to air (oxygen) while they are overheating, there will be a fire resembling magnesium fire.

According to many nuclear experts a zirconium fire would probably release most of the radioactivity inside the nuclear fuel rods into the atmosphere in the form of a highly radioactive aerosol, consisting of small and nanoparticles. Most of the radioactive impurities produced by the neutron bombardment inside the reactor are created relatively close to the surface of the fuel rod, because neutrons do not penetrate deep inside a fuel rod that consists of heavy metals.

Moreover, a zirconium fire and the residual heat generated by the spontaneous decay of the radioactive impurities in the nuclear fuel can together produce more than enough heat energy to vaporize at least part if not most of the uranium and plutonium oxides inside the fuel rods.

The specific heat capacity of uranium is 0.12 joules per gram. This means that we need only 0.12 joules of energy to raise the temperature of one gram of uranium by one degree Celsius (or by one degree Kelvin). One joule is the amount of energy that is consumed when we spend one watt of energy for one second.

About 0.12 joules per gram is a very low specific heat capacity. The specific heat capacity of water is 4 joules per gram, 33 times more. In other words, the amount of energy that can increase the temperature of a ton of water by 1 degree can raise the temperature of a ton of uranium by 33 degrees.

Pure uranium melts at a relatively low temperature, at 1,135 degrees Celsius. However, it vaporizes only at 4,130 degrees Celsius. Besides this, to melt a gram of uranium 38 joules is needed, and to vaporize it, either 1750 or 2025 joules (the sources I have found seem to disagree on this).

As I said, the uranium in nuclear fuel has been burned to uranium oxide, to prevent it from catching fire in high temperatures. An added benefit is that uranium oxide does not melt at 1,135 degrees like pure uranium, but only at 2,870 degrees. On the other hand, it vaporizes in a lower temperature than pure uranium, at 3,540 degrees. According to the sources I have found 275 joules of energy is needed to melt and about 2,000 joules to vaporize a gram of uranium oxide.

It is more difficult to find the same figures for plutonium oxides or MOX, but I have been told that the numbers are roughly in the same range than those for uranium oxide.

It takes 333 joules to melt a gram of ice and 2260 joules to vaporize a gram of water. In other words, you need less energy to melt a ton of uranium oxide than you need to melt a ton of ice. Similarly, less energy is needed for vaporizing a ton of uranium oxide than for vaporizing a ton of water.

Besides this, the difference between the melting point and vaporizing point of uranium oxide is only 675 degrees Celsius (!).

Thanks to Harrisburg and Fukushima we know that it is not difficult to melt a nuclear reactor. Actually, in a crises situation, it seems to be rather hard to prevent the nuclear fuel from melting. But after the fuel has melted, we only need 675 more degrees to vaporize at least part of it.

In an old-fashioned nuclear reactor which contains 120 tons of nuclear fuel, we would need about 300 billion joules to vaporize the fuel (all of it) minus the heat that is conducted or radiated away, cooling the fuel.

If the nuclear fuel kept producing 2 megawatts of residual heat per ton per hour after the reactor shut-down, 120 tons of nuclear fuel would produce 900 billion joules of energy during the first hour, three times more than were needed for vaporize all the fuel.

In reality, the production of heat is much less, because the amount of residual heat produced by a nuclear reactor drops from 7 per cent to 2 per cent of what is produced while the reactor is operating, during the first hour after the reactor shut-down. In spite of this the amount of residual heat should still be enough to vaporize much of the fuel, in suitable conditions.

And if the reactor core is exposed to air so that the zirconium cladding ignites, burning zirconium will add more heat into the process.

In other words: I do not think that we can really exclude the possibility that much if not most of the radioactivity inside a nuclear reactor might be released in a very serious accident.

In the European Pressurized Water Reactors (EPR) of Areva nuclear fuel will be hotter and produce even more residual heat after the reactor has stopped. This might raise the stakes and risks to an even higher level.

In the EPRs nuclear fuel will be kept inside for a much longer time than in the old models. The idea is to increase the burn-up rate or the amount of energy that can be extracted from the fuel from 20 Gwd/tU (gigawatt-days of power per one tonne of uranium fuel) to 60 Gwd/tU. Critical nuclear experts have commented for me, in informal discussions, that this might triple the peak amount of radioactivity and residual heat in the nuclear fuel. Unfortunately, I have not been able to verify this claim. I have enquired about this both from Areva (the supplier of the EPRs) and from Teollisuuden Voima (the Finnish buyer of Areva's first EPR) but they have refused to answer the question. When I have sent e-mails about the subject they always say that we will come back to this later, but I never hear about them again. Similarly, when I have met their representatives in seminars or in hearings in the Finnish parliament, and tried to enquire about the subject, they just turn their backs to me and walk away. This gives a strong impression that they have something to hide.

I once got close to getting an answer to the question. I was invited to testify in the economic sub-committee of the Finnish parliament, concerning whether Finland should give permits for the nuclear power companies to construct one, two or three more nuclear power stations. Three other witnesses had been invited to the same session: Teollisuuden Voima and Fennovoima, the companies that had submitted requests to construct two more nuclear power plants, and Posiva, the Finnish company that is excavating a deep cave system for storing Finland's used nuclear fuel.

In the discussion Päivi Lipponen, a social democratic member of the Finnish parliament (and the wife of Paavo Lipponen, a former prime minister of Finland) enquired whether the higher amount of residual heat and radioactivity in the EPR reactor could be an extra security risk.

I thought that now they finally have to say something, because you are obliged to answer the questions put forward by MPs in a parliamentary hearing, but I once again underestimated the level of cunning of nuclear industry representatives. Teollisuuden Voima and Fennovoima remained silent and let the representative of Posiva answer the question. The Posiva man said that yes, nuclear fuel from EPR would be hotter than the fuel coming from earlier reactor types. But that only means that it has to be kept in a cooling pond for a few decades longer before it can be transported into a permanent storage inside the deep cave system, Onkalo, which was true, but besides the point. Ms Lipponen did not know enough about the matter to pose a follow-up question by herself. I tried to intervene but wasn't given the possibility to do that because the members of the committee were in a hurry and closed the session.

However, the answer by the Posiva representative kind of confirmed what I had been told, before. If the nuclear fuel coming from EPR is so much hotter that it has to be kept in a cooling pond for a few extra decades, it must also produce more residual heat when taken out of the reactor, and this can only be if it is more radioactive than ordinary spent nuclear fuel.

So the nuclear fuel of an EPR might actually contain more than 100,000 curies or 4,000 terabecquerels of radioactivity after it has been in use for some time. I hasten to add that this is only an informed guess provided by critical nuclear experts that do not want to be publicly quoted. The figure I have quoted may be wrong, to an extent, but I have to use it because Areva and Teollisuuden Voima have refused to provide the accurate number. Which actually implies that the reality might be even worse.

At least some of the breeder reactors (thorium reactors) planned by India could be even more dangerous, because they have a positive (and not a negative) coolant void coefficient. This means that in these reactor types the amount of heat produced by a reactor actually grows for some time after the reactor has lost its coolant and shut down.

So, theoretically, a nuclear reactor might release, according to the worst-case-scenario, even a few tens of billions of curies of radioactivity into the atmosphere, in the form of small and nanoparticles.

This amount will, of course, diminish very quickly, at least in the very beginning. If 70 billion curies were released immediately after the reactor shut-down, this will be reduced to 20 billion curies within the first hour, to 4 billion curies in 24 hours and to 1 billion curies in a week. The bad news is that after the first week the amount of radioactivity, counted as curies, only declines slowly. Painfully, excruciatingly slowly.

And a billion curies is still a huge, mind-boggling amount. The bodies of the seven billion human beings now living on earth together contain slightly more than a thousand curies of radioactivity, most of that in the form of radioactive potassium lodged inside our bones.

6

What Could Cause a Major Radioactive Release?

There are a number of factors that could devastate nuclear power facilities and release huge amounts of radioactive pollution into the atmosphere.

We learnt in Fukushima that a large tsunami wave hitting numerous coastal nuclear power plants, their cooling ponds and nuclear fuel recycling facilities at the same time is a very real possibility.

Even in the North Atlantic there has been roughly one 10-15-metre-high tsunami in a century. The most recent such events have taken place during years 1580, 1607, 1755 and 1929.

Strikes by asteroids or comet fragments and major submarine landslides can cause even larger tsunamis, known as megatsunamis.

The collapse of an old volcano can also produce an extremely large tsunami wave. In Hawaii there are traces of tsunamis six hundred metres above the sea level. In the Canary islands Tenerife, El Hierro and La Palma have produced a number of very large landslides. Probably the largest one took place in Tenerife, where a very large chunk of the mountain slid into the sea, cutting the height of El

Teide—or, more precisely, Mt Tenerife—from roughly six kilometres to the present 3.8 kilometres. The submarine landslide is roughly 250 kilometres long, and the largest single boulders lying at the bottom of the sea are kilometres across still one hundred kilometres from Tenerife.

The island of La Palma consists of two clearly separate peaks. This is because the island is slowly splitting apart. According to geologists the next major eruption on the island might cause the southern half of the island, known as Cumbre Vieja or the Old Mountain to slide into the sea. If 500 or 1,000 cubic kilometres of volcanic rock splashed into the water, a truly huge tsunami would be created. According to researchers it would start as a 650-metre-high tidal wave and hit the eastern coast of the United States as a 50- or 100-metre-high tsunami.

Global warming may further increase the incidence of very large tsunami events via a number of different mechanisms.

The researchers of the Christian Albrecht University in Kiel, Germany and the Shirshov Institute for Oceanographic Research in Moscow have noted that global warming may cause large tsunamis by destabilizing offshore methane clathrate beds. Methane clathrates are ice-like solids in which methane molecules have been trapped inside molecular-level cages that consist of ordinary ice. Clathrates are only stable in high-pressure conditions that exist under more than two hundred metres of water and in temperatures only a couple of degrees above the freezing point of water. About 7,900 years ago a large eruption of methane from clathrates off the coast of Norway triggered a vast submarine avalanche of mud, rock and other loose sediments, known as the Storegga, or the Great Wall. The

Storegga submarine landslide also caused a very large tsunami at the coastal areas of Britain and Norway.

There are about 6,000 cubic kilometres of debris in the Storegga area. According to the present assessment, there have been many different landslides, the largest one of which—the one that took place 7,900 years ago—consisted of approximately 1,700 cubic kilometres of sediments. The researchers of the Tromsö University have said that there is one submarine cliff off the coast of Norway—four times taller than Storegga—that might be destabilized by the melting of the clathrates.

A much smaller, 200-cubic kilometre underwater landslide or "turbidity flow" in 1929 caused a relatively large tsunami at the coastal areas of Newfoundland, Canada. The tsunami was seven metres high on large stretches of coastline but rose to 27 metres at bays which concentrated its energy.

The disintegration of continental ice sheets can also trigger vast tsunamis. A continental ice sheet weighs so much, that the earth's crust under it is often depressed by more than a kilometre. When the glacier begins to melt it becomes lighter and the crust starts to bounce back. This can create very large rebound earthquakes and related tsunamis.

The melting of the Fennoscandian ice sheet, which lay over Finland, Sweden and Norway during the last Ice Age, took thousands of years. In spite of this the melting created a few very strong and innumerable smaller earthquakes. The largest earthquakes in Sweden had a magnitude of at least 8.5 or 8.7 on the Richter scale, and possibly much more. They caused at least 13 large tsunamis at the Baltic Sea, many of which were 20 metres high and some of which probably reached the height of 30 or 40 metres.

If an ice sheet loses much of its weight in, for example, two hundred years, the resulting earthquakes will inevitably be much more violent than when the process takes place in 4,000 or 6,000 years. In the worst case scenario a gigantic chunk of an ice sheet anchored below the sea level might suddenly slide into the ocean and just float away. This is the most serious possibility, because the weight depressing the crust would be lifted in almost instantly, in a geological blink of an eye. (I used this scenario in a science fiction novel, *The Sands of Sarasvati.*)

The scenario may sound far-fetched, but we actually know that something like this must have happened at the end of the last Ice Age. Marine scientists have discovered large furrows at the sea bottom, at a depth of two kilometres. The furrows had been carved by enormous icebergs, which can only have been chunks of whole, fragmented ice sheets.

Scientists of the University of Wollongong have found traces of huge megatsunamis from the coastal areas of Australia. Some had reached 35 kilometres inland and deposited car-sized boulders 130 metres above the present sea level. Most of them have probably been caused by the melting of the Antarctic ice sheet at the end of the last Ice Age.

The latest megatsunami, which took place in the 1430s, was probably caused by a small asteroid or a comet fragment. It reached the maximum height of 220 metres in New Zealand, 130 metres in Australia and 25 metres in Canada, at the other side of the Pacific.

The forces created by a wave do not increase in a linear way. Everyone who has swum in the Pacific knows that while a one-metre-high breaking wave is not a problem, a two-metre-high breaker can kill you, if you are careless. A 20-metre-high breaking wave already hits with the force of six kilograms per square centimetre, or sixty tons per square metre, not to say anything about a 130-metre- or 220-metre-high supergiant.

A tsunami can disrupt the primary and secondary cooling systems of a nuclear power plant by flooding engine rooms, by damaging fuel pipes or by washing fuel tanks away (like in Fukushima). Besides this, the withdrawing wave could bury the mouths of cooling pipes under ten metres of sand and other debris, so that water can no longer get through. For instance, the tsunami wave that hit the Portuguese, Spanish and Moroccan coasts in 1755 produced very impressive lagoon systems and sand dunes when the water withdrew, taking a lot of sand with it.

Above all, the primary cooling system of a nuclear power plant always uses grid power. A nuclear reactor cannot produce electric power for its own cooling systems, it can only feed huge amounts of power into the grid and take some of that back from the grid. If the electric grid goes down, nuclear power plants shut down automatically, but at the same time they also lose the primary power source of their cooling system.

Even if the diesel engines powering the secondary cooling systems remained operational and the supply of cooling water were not interrupted, nuclear power plants have not prepared themselves for long power cuts. Most of them only have diesel fuel for a couple of days. In Finland nuclear power plants have diesel oil for three days, in the USA for seven days. This is not a very long time because—as I already mentioned—the nuclear fuel rods in the reactors and inside the cooling ponds have to be water-cooled for decades even after the reactor has shut down, to prevent the feared zirconium fire or a full-scale melt down of the reactor.

As we saw in Fukushima, a large tsunami can definitely disrupt the power grid. This means that a very large tsunami could disable the primary cooling systems of even the nuclear power plants constructed far inland, by disrupting the supply of grid power. Even if the secondary systems remained operational, the nuclear fuel would catch fire soon after the diesel fuel had run out, unless somebody managed to bring more fuel for the secondary cooling systems, in spite of the general chaos. In the coastal areas the tank trucks bringing the fuel would also have to get through the mountains of debris and devastation left behind the tsunami.

In 2006 five Finnish members of the European parliament—Anneli Jäätteenmäki, Alexander Stubb, Satu Hassi, Riitta Muller and Esko Seppänen—drafted a proposal urging the European Union to check whether European nuclear power plants on coastal areas had adequate defences against tsunamis and flood waves caused by hurricanes or lesser storms. The proposal was adopted by the environmental committee of the European Parliament by 31 votes for and 20 against. Unfortunately, the majority of the members of the European parliament (MEPs) representing conservative, populist and extreme rightist parties voted against the notion, so that the proposal was defeated in the plenary on February 14, 2007, by 286 votes for and 373 against. In other words, the European Parliament decided, in February 2007, that tsunamis cannot constitute a threat for coastal nuclear facilities and that the adequacy of European nuclear power stations' sea defences should not be investigated (!).

The conservatives were probably afraid that a check-up would increase the production costs of nuclear power and nuclear experts assured them that even a very large tsunami could never do any harm for a nuclear power plant.

After Fukushima, the behaviour of the nuclear experts —and of the European right-wing parties—of course seemed astonishingly irresponsible. After Fukushima everybody knows that even a relatively small tsunami can cause a very serious situation in a nuclear power plant.

We should remember that Japan was not the worst-prepared nuclear power producing country. On the contrary, it was probably the only country in the world which had prepared itself for tsunamis that might one day strike at its coastal nuclear power plants. Unlike the nuclear power plants of other countries, Japan's coastal nuclear facilities did have sea defences, protective walls that were meant to break or at least reduce the strength of a tsunami wave.

In practice it turned out that the Japanese sea defences were not adequate to break even a relatively small tsunami. But if something similar had happened in another country whose nuclear power plants had no sea defences at all, the results might have been much worse.

Tsunamis, unfortunately, are only one of numerous frightening possibilities.

A large number of other factors could also destroy power grids for months, for years, or even for decades. A war or a series of carefully targeted terrorist strikes targeting the nerve centres of the power grid could do this. A large earthquake or the ash fall from a major volcanic eruption could destroy both the power lines and the transformers. Even a major plasma pulse, a geomangnetic storm from the sun could fry our grids.

According to the British government, there are two potential mega-catastrophes or mega-threats which have a much higher probability of becoming true than the other theoretically possible nightmare scenarios. One is a new influenza pandemic and the other is a major geomagnetic storm, strong enough to fry our electric power grids. According to the UK government, the probability of the latter kind of event becoming a reality is 12 per cent per decade. The estimate is based on radioactive beryllium anomalies in ice cores cut from the Greenland and Antarctic ice sheets.

Such huge plasma pulses have last hit the earth in 1921 and 1859. They are known as Carrington events, according to Richard Carrington, the British amateur astronomer who produced the best report of the 1859 event.

Recent reports by Nasa, the National Academy of Science of the USA and the US Congress have estimated, that if a new Carrington event hit the earth today, it could destroy 350 extremely-high-voltage or EHV transformers in the USA and 2,000 worldwide. This would mean that almost every power grid on the planet might fall down for years, if not decades, because the current world production of EHV transformers is about one hundred per year, and the factories producing them would also lose their power with the grid. In the US debate it has been observed, that a new Carrington event could—in theory—produce 400 Chernobyls, or a Fukushima-like crises situation simultaneously in most or all of the world's four hundred nuclear power plants.

If we want to keep producing electricity by nuclear power, a certain minimum requirement should be to equip nuclear power plants with windmills, solar panels and thermoelectric cells that could produce auxiliary power for the cooling systems in the case of a long grid failure. Unfortunately, we have not done so, yet.

It seems that in the International Atomic Energy Association there has never been a proper, serious and detailed discussion about nuclear safety during power cuts that would last several years or decades and create a chaotic situation that might disrupt the transportation of diesel fuel for the secondary power sources of the cooling systems.

The prevailing attitude seems to be that it is enough to store diesel fuel for the auxiliary systems for a few days, because for example, fire engines can soon bring more fuel for the nuclear power plants. Alternatively power can be transmitted along the old, auxiliary 150 kilovolt transmission lines.

Can We be Certain that It Would Go Like This?

It is true that most countries have also preserved at least some of the older and smaller power transmission lines. They could, at least in theory, be used to transport electricity for many nuclear power plants in the case of a serious emergency. During a prolonged grid failure all other users of power—factories, company offices, government and municipal buildings, individual households—could be disconnected so that all available power could be channelled for the cooling systems of nuclear reactors.

However, if a Carrington event has fried the large high-voltage transformers, this power should be first channelled to numerous small transformers and then from them to the nuclear power plants. Can this be done automatically, if the internet and telephone networks are not operating? Who can give the orders for the people operating the smaller transformers, transmission lines and power plants? What if some of the persons needed for doing something have left to check whether their families or their old parents are all right?

What if key people just run away, fearing a major radiation leakage? In Fukushima the personnel of the nuclear power stations that were in danger almost escaped and ran away to save their lives, which might have produced an accident hundreds of times worse than what actually happened. Only a direct order by the Japanese Prime Minister to stay stopped them from running away. What if there is no way to deliver a strong message from the prime minister or the president for the workers on all key sites?

What if the problem were not caused by a Carrington event but by a huge earthquake or by a heavy ash fall from major volcanic eruption? Heavy volcanic ash fall would damage or destroy both the larger and the smaller power transmission lines and transformers at the same time.

What if the fire engines bringing more diesel oil for the nuclear power plants will not be able to get through because the roads have been damaged by an earthquake or because they cannot be used due to a blizzard (because nobody has cleared the snow away), volcanic ash fall or debris piled by a large tsunami?

What if the drivers of fire engines or oil trucks are worried about their families, or just too scared to approach a nuclear power plant that is "about to blow up"?

IAEA and the national nuclear safety authorities have

not discussed and analysed any of these possibilities. They should do so.

Combined Effects of Sea Level Rise, Storm Surges and Tsunamis

It is important to realize, that when we are discussing the safety of coastal nuclear power complexes we should also pay attention to the combined effects of the predicted rise in sea level and tsunamis or storm surges created by unprecedentedly fierce hurricanes and typhoons.

According to the current official prediction by IPCC (Intergovernmental Panel on Climate Change) the sea level is only likely to rise by a metre or so during this century, due to the heat expansion of sea water and because of the melting of ice sheets and mountain glaciers. This estimate is slightly higher than IPCC's earlier assessment, which said that the sea level would only rise by 20-65 centimetres before the year 2100.

However, at the moment the sea level is already rising by almost 4 millimetres a year, which would amount to 40 centimetres in a century. Four millimetres per year is not yet a catastrophic speed, but at the beginning of the 20th century and during the centuries that preceded it the average rate of sea level rise only was about 0.1 millimetres per year, forty times less. Nobody can say how the process will continue in the future, but we have, in a surprisingly short period of time, proceeded from 0.1 millimetres per year to uncomfortably close of the higher end of IPCC's former prediction.

Nasa's James Hansen, one of the world's most respected climate scientists says that the figures put forward by IPCC are probably far too low. According to Hansen, it is more likely that the sea level will rise by five metres or something like that during the next one hundred years.

Hansen's estimate is based on climatic history and not on computer models, on the fact that natural warming of climate has occasionally been able to raise the sea level by more than 20 metres in 400 years, meaning more than five metres per century.

The naturally occurring, climate-warming radiative forcings were much smaller than what humanity has already produced. We are now heating the globe by increasing the atmosphere's greenhouse gas concentrations, by producing extra cirrus clouds that have a strong warming impact and by producing very high amounts of soot, tar particles and dust that rain on the continental ice sheets, mountain glaciers and other snow and ice fields. Besides this there is a growing amount of micro-algae growing on the surface of the ice sheets because of the nitrogen oxides and other nutrients raining down on the ice.

Soot, tar, dead algae and dust reduce the reflectivity of ice and snow so that it absorbs a growing percentage of solar radiation. Shining white, fresh-fallen snow can reflect up to 98 per cent of all solar radiation straight back to space, but grey, dirty snow absorbs most of it.

Hansen's point is that if we are now heating the ice sheets much more forcefully than nature was able to do, can we really be sure that the ice will still melt five times slower than the maximum natural speed, and not with equal or greater speed?

If we construct nuclear power plants on coastal areas, we should also prepare for a scenario in which the sea level rises by at least five metres during the next one hundred years. This means that if we want to protect nuclear facilities against 30-metre-high tsunamis we have to construct them at least 35 metres above the current sea level.

Another, related issue are the temporary floods or storm surges caused by typhoons and hurricanes. According to the Saffir-Simpson scale of major storms a category five typhoon (or a category five hurricane) is a cyclone in which prevailing winds exceed 250 metres per second and which produces a storm surge with a minimal height of five and a half metres. In bays that concentrate the energy of the flood the five and a half metres can sometimes mean twenty-five metres or more.

Practically all climate scientists agree that a warmer climate will produce stronger storms. The fuel of hurricanes and typhoons is the water vapour that evaporates from the sea and then rises higher in the atmosphere. When it again condenses to water it releases its latent heat into the air. The maximum amount of water the air can contain is a function of temperature, which means that the higher the temperature, the more water vapour there can be in the air and the stronger hurricanes and typhoons can be produced.

If the world warms by 2, 4 or 6 centigrades, tropical seas will be able to produce more powerful storms than before and we may have to add category six in the Saffir-Simpson scale.

The designers of coastal nuclear power plants should also remember, that the rise in sea level and the storm surges can both shift the zone where the wind-generated waves break. If we construct a nuclear power plant on a bay where a storm surge can raise the water by twenty metres, so that it reaches the bottom of the reactor buildings, the huge waves generated by the hurricane winds can travel on top of this bed of water without breaking before the buildings. In such a situation reactor buildings and the pipe and power lines outside them would become breakers.

As I have already mentioned, a twenty-metre-high breaking wave generates a pressure of sixty tons per square metre. During the Second World War, this was enough to bend thick steel baulks and to crush the steel plates of powerful modern warships. Would all the relevant structures of a nuclear facility stand, without becoming seriously damaged, thousands or tens of thousands of blows struck by a watery hammer hitting with the force of sixty tons per square metre? Keeping in mind the devastation caused by a single tsunami wave in Fukushima, it is hard to believe that all the pipes, doors and valves could survive such continuous punishment.

If we want to construct nuclear power plants in coastal areas, their designers should always make the following calculation:

> The lowest allowable height from the sea level of a planned coastal nuclear power plant = A + B + C + D, where
>
> A = the largest potentially possible amount of sea level rise, due to the heat expansion of water and the melting of the ice sheets during the operational age of the planned facility
>
> B = the highest potentially possible storm surge that could be caused by cyclones, typhoons or hurricanes in the area (assuming a four-degree rise in global average temperatures)
>
> C = the height of the wind-generated waves that can travel over the water bed created by the highest possible storm surge

D = the height of the breakers that would be created by the wind-generated waves travelling over the flood and hitting the structures of the nuclear power plant (= in Fukushima the oil tanks were ripped off when the tsunami wave struck against the reactor building and the resulting surge of water, essentially a breaker, washed over the building's roof).

Terrorist Strikes Against Power Complexes

A terrorist strike—or a series of terrorist strikes—against nuclear power complexes is also an issue that ought to be taken very seriously. This could really happen, one day.

After the terrorist strikes to Washington and New York on September 11, 2001, two al-Qaida leaders then based in Pakistan, Khaled al-Sheikh Mohammad and Ramzi bin al-Shaibab, told al-Jazeera in Karachi that the original plan had been to crash the planes on US nuclear power stations. The plan was changed because al-Qaida leaders decided that the results from a nuclear strike might be too unpredictable. Al-Qaida leaders thought they only had the right to kill six million Americans to revenge the six million Muslims who had died—according to their calculations—because of the USA.

The second generation of al-Qaida leaders, however, was less moderate. One of its key members, Abu Musab al-Zarqawi, revealed that the long-term plan of the younger al-Qaida leaders was to use weapons of mass destruction and strikes against nuclear power plants in order to destroy the world's pagan civilizations, so that after the war only one billion Muslims remained alive and six billion people had died.

Al-Qaida is no longer doing so well and will not be able to kill six billion non-Muslim people. However, the serious point is that some other terrorist organizations might one day make a serious attack against one or more nuclear power complexes, if we keep producing electricity with nuclear power. We should prepare ourselves for such attacks and do our utmost to ensure that they cannot succeed.

Representatives of nuclear power companies and the national nuclear safety authorities often produce astonishingly optimistic assessments about the possible consequences of a serious terrorist strike against a nuclear reactor. But, for instance, the US Air Forces—which, in this case, might be a more reliable source of information—have produced drastically different figures.

According to a study (Nichelson-Medlin-Stafford: Radiological Weapons of Terror) by three generals of the US Air Forces, terrorists could kill most of the unprotected population of Washington DC, New York, Baltimore and Philadelphia if they acquired ten kilograms of used nuclear fuel just taken out from a reactor, and vaporized it with a ton of conventional high explosive. Such a dirty bomb of three million curies or so would greatly increase cancer mortality along the whole East Coast of the USA.

What if terrorists vaporized all the nuclear fuel in a big reactor, or in two, four, eight or twenty reactors? Three thousand tonnes of used nuclear fuel instead of ten kilograms as in the Nichelson-Medlin-Stafford scenario!

A few years ago, I had a few high-profile public debates about the issue with Jukka Laaksonen, the former Director-General of the Finnish Nuclear Safety Center, and the present director of Rosatom's foreign sales department. Rosatom, Russia's state-owned nuclear power company, is now actively trying to promote nuclear power and its own reactors in a large number of countries, including India.

Laaksonen said that the three US generals and the Staff College (a military academy) of the US Air Forces had exaggerated the danger and that the ensuing radioactive fallout would be three million times less dangerous than the US Air Forces had estimated. So in reality it would be likely that no one would be killed or seriously injured, even if terrorists fried a couple of nuclear reactors.

I must say I was somewhat taken aback by Laaksonen's comment, but I had to admire his self-confidence. How could he be so totally convinced that his own calculations were correct and that everybody in the US military had bought a figure that was three million times too large?

I countered by remarking, that the US military definitely knows more about RDD weapons (Radioactivity Dispersal Devices) and other radiation weapons than anyone else.

The US military became genuinely worried when Hitler became interested in radiation weapons during the final years of the Second World War. Hitler commanded his scientists to investigate, whether it would be possible to prevent the invasion of Western Allies with radiation weapons, or dirty bombs covering much of Belgium, the Netherlands and France with highly radioactive substances. Owing to the influence of Air Marshall Curtis LeMay, US Air Forces launched a serious research programme related to radiation weapons.

During the Second World War Curtis LeMay was responsible for the terror bombing of Japan. He also inspired the character of a mad air colonel in Stanley Kubrick's classic film *Doctor Strangelove.*

During the Korean war, the USA considered spraying

radioactive waste from plutonium reprocessing plants across Korea to create a "dehumanized death belt". The congressman who proposed the radioactive death belt was Albert Gore, father of the former vice president and climate campaigner Al Gore.

USA even exploded one relatively large dirty bomb, the Castle Bravo which I have already mentioned. Its detonation produced an extremely lethal radioactive cloud which made the inhabitants of two coral islands—Utrik and Rongelap—so ill that they had to be evacuated in order to save their lives. Utrik and Rongelap were three hundred and five hundred kilometres from the Ground Zero. Castle Bravo contained hundreds of times less radioactive material than a big nuclear reactor.

For these reasons I thought that the US military was better informed about the possibilities and problems related to radioactivity dispersal devices than Laaksonen. After all, Finland's Nuclear Safety Center had never been able to conduct empirical experiments with them, unlike the US military.

Laaksonen countered by saying that the whole scenario presented by Medlin, Nichelson and Stafford did not make any sense. If a group of terrorists somehow managed to extract a ten-kilogram nuclear fuel rod from a nuclear reactor, the mere gamma radiation produced by the rod would kill them in a few minutes.

At this point Laaksonen's logic became somewhat difficult for me to follow. If the mere external gamma radiation from a single, ten-kilogram nuclear fuel rod were enough to kill a group of terrorists in a matter of minutes, why would a terrorist strike vaporizing for instance 160,000 similar fuel rods into a highly radioactive cloud of aerosols not be a threat to anyone?

If we continue to produce electricity with nuclear power, the reactors should be constructed deep underground, inside the bedrock, so that they cannot blow their contents into the atmosphere, in any circumstances. Even Edward Teller, one of the fathers of the hydrogen bomb, thought that this would be the proper and sane thing to do.

The containment shields of the already existing nuclear reactors should be strengthened so that they can withstand a rapid series of three or four separate strikes by large passenger jets, as well as attacks carried out with bunker-buster missiles like the "Deep Digger". Coastal nuclear power stations should be equipped with improved sea defences. Also the cooling ponds storing used nuclear fuel should be equipped with proper containment shields and heavily safeguarded. At least some national army, navy and air force units should be concentrated near the nuclear power complexes. Electric fences and infra-red alarm systems should be installed around the reactor sites, and especially the actual reactor buildings should be re-designed by military experts and equipped with a set of manned strong points with sufficient fields of fire, so that they can act as formidable fortresses against possible commando strikes by terrorists. There should always be armed security guards or soldiers inside the actual reactor building.

Kite power stations should perhaps be constructed on the no-fly zones surrounding the nuclear power complexes, in order to prevent a strike with an aeroplane or with a glider. The protection of the primary cooling pipes should be improved so that they cannot be destroyed, for example, by small portable missiles or with rocket-propelled grenades

(RPGs). Primary cooling pipes should be guarded against a terrorist strike by divers using aqualungs. The computer systems of the nuclear power plants should be protected against flux compressors, other kinds of microwave bombs, Marx impulse generators and other EMP weapons according to the best currently available military standards.

The US nuclear power complexes now employ 75 armed guards in four shifts, meaning altogether 300 armed security guards on the pay-list. This should perhaps be seen as the minimum requirement in other countries, as well. Of course, the main responsibility for guarding nuclear power plants against terrorist attacks lies with the US Air Forces, Navy and Army, the police and the various secret security organizations, which currently employ more than one million people in the USA, according to recently published estimates.

7

The Promise of Fusion

We often hear that in the long run we can replace the "dirty" fission-based nuclear energy with "clean" fusion-based nuclear power. Fusion is the ultimate way of generating electricity, because a fusion reactor produces clean energy and no waste, and uses seawater as its fuel.

In reality there are three different fusion reactor concepts: deuterium-tritium fusion reactor (the one that is being developed), helium 3-helium 3 fusion reactor (that could produce clean energy) and deuterium-deuterium fusion reactor (that could, in a way, be powered with mere sea water).

It is important to realize that the Fusion Power Plant of our dreams—the fusion reactor that uses sea water as its fuel and does not produce any dangerous pollution—is a purely imaginary concept that does not exist even as a theoretical concept. This Dream Plant liberally combines the best qualities of all three existing fusion power concepts and ignores their problematic charasteristics. This can be done in the nuclear dream world, but not in the real universe.

Deuterium-tritium Fusion Power Plants

ITER (International Thermonuclear Experimental Reactor), the joint fusion power project of Japan, USA and the European Union, has been hailed as an effort to produce safe and non-polluting nuclear energy. We are being told that such fusion reactors would not produce any dangerous radioactive waste, unlike present nuclear power plants. It is also said that in ITER-type fusion power plants it is not necessary to deal with dangerous radioactive substances like plutonium and uranium and that a fusion reactor would use seawater as its "fuel". All these statements are quite misleading.

In practice ITER would "burn" lithium 6, broken down to tritium, and deuterium. As mentioned above, tritium and deuterium are not exactly harmless substances, they are the main ingredients in hydrogen and hydrogen-uranium bombs (fission-fusion bombs and fission-fusion-fission bombs). Tritium is approximately half a billion times more radioactive than uranium 238. It is used as the trigger in many ordinary fission bombs, and a few grams of tritium or lithium 6 and deuterium multiplies the explosive strength of an ordinary fission bomb.

As mentioned in the preceding chapters, the easiest way to make a truly massive atomic bomb is to use some lithium 6, some deuterium (which can be distilled from sea water), 270 grams of very pure uranium 235 or a slightly smaller amount of plutonium—and a lot of natural uranium. The explosion of the uranium 235 or plutonium 239 core triggers fusion reactions in the second phase of the bomb, consisting of lithium 6 and deuterium. This produces so much heat and neutrons that if the core of the bomb is surrounded by a thick mantle of ordinary uranium 238 (or natural uranium), many of the uranium 238 atoms will split, even though uranium 238 cannot experience a proper chain reaction.

Moreover, an ITER-type fusion power plant would most probably produce a larger quantity of highly radioactive nuclear waste than an ordinary nuclear power plant. ITER would not produce used nuclear fuel rods, but the whole mantle of the plant becomes very radioactive and has to be changed at least once in a few years, possibly even more often than this.

The material of the mantle then becomes highly radioactive and dangerous nuclear waste, and there will be a lot of it.

The problem arises from the fact that the fusion of deuterium and tritium produces neutrons and not protons. Since neutrons do not have an electric charge it is not possible to direct them by strong magnetic fields, which means that they hit the reactor's mantle and make it very radioactive.

Nuclear fuel of an ordinary nuclear power station has typically become almost one billion times more radioactive when it comes out from the reactor, because of the induced or artificial radioactivity, radioactive impurities created by the intensive neutron bombardment inside the reactor. Neutrons created by deuterium-tritium fusion do the same thing for the mantle of a fusion power plant.

Helium 3 Fusion Power Plants

A fusion power plant based on the reaction of two helium 3 atoms would not produce much radioactive waste because helium 3-helium 3-fusion produces protons which have a positive electric charge and which can therefore be steered by magnetic fields. However, the nearest significant sources of helium 3 are the solar wind, the moon (whose loose sediments contain up to 20 parts per billion of helium 3) and the atmospheres of Jupiter and Saturn.

A research team at the University of Wisconsin (USA) has calculated that mining of the moon's helium 3 reserves for fusion power plants might become economically feasible if we can reduce the price of delivering equipment on the moon's surface to USD 1,000 per kilogram. Apollo flights delivered material to the moon with slightly less than two million dollars per kilogram. Advances in rocket, space tether and solar technologies may change these equations, but they are not likely to make lunar helium 3 mining economical compared with the new photovoltaic, geothermal and wind power technologies.

Deuterium-deuterium Fusion Power Plants

It would, at least in theory, also be possible to construct a fusion reactor that would only use seawater or, more precisely, only deuterium as its fuel. In the ocean one water molecule in six thousand is heavy water, and contains one atom of deuterium and one atom of ordinary hydrogen instead of two ordinary hydrogen atoms.

In reality nobody is interested in seawater fusion power plants, except in speeches meant for politicians, journalists and the public.

It is true that the fusion of two deuterium atoms has a fifty per cent chance of producing a neutron and a fifty per cent chance of making a proton. Besides this the secondary reactions emit some more neutrons, but the production of neutrons is still much less than with tritium-deuterium fusion.

The problem is that the fusion of two deuterium atoms produces only 3,65 MeV (megaelectronvolts) of energy, while the fusion of deuterium and tritium provides 17,6 MeV and the fusion of two helium 3 atoms 12,9 MeV. Thus a seawater reactor would produce even more radioactive waste for each megawatt-hour of energy than a tritium-deuterium plant. You can't get much farther from the dream of clean nuclear energy!

The Economic Feasibility of Fusion

What about the economic feasibility of fusion power? How close are we to an economic breakthrough, after which fusion power can compete with other forms of power production without subsidies?

Don't hold your breath while waiting!

The world's most advanced experimental fusion reactor is called NIF, National Ignition Facility, in Lawrence Livermore National Laboratory, in the state of California in the USA. The central element of NIF is a huge battery of 192 powerful lasers. The array is 215 metres long and 120 metres wide, or roughly the size of Colosseum. Its original construction budget was 3.5 billion dollars, but the real expenditure has been much higher. On top of this come the salaries of NIF's 850 engineers and scientists.

NIF is closer to making the dream of fusion to come true than ITER or any other fusion research centre in the world. Its 192 lasers can produce enormously powerful pulses of energy that can be directed very accurately towards the same spot, so that the implosion of deuterium and tritium can heat the gas to one hundred million degrees and force hydrogen atoms to fuse. The power output of the laser battery can, for brief moments, exceed the combined power of all power-producing facilities of the United States of America by a factor of five hundred.

The final aim is to create fusion reactions that produced 15 times more energy than is needed to initiate them.

Presented like this, it does not—actually—sound so bad.

But, remember: fusion researchers are nuclear scientists. Like other types of nuclear scientists, they never tell the whole truth, but only small and very carefully selected bits and pieces of the truth.

They do not like to mention, that the laser pulses that can be produced are not only somewhat short but extremely short. They do not last hours or minutes, but one-third of a billionth of a second, after which it takes several hours before the laser battery can fire the next pulse.

This means that even though the capacity of the lasers can "temporarily", meaning for one-third of a billionth of a second, exceed the electricity production capacity of all power plants in the USA by five hundred times, the average power of the lasers is only about one hundred watts, the equivalent of an ordinary light bulb.

In other words, if NIF achieves its goals and produces 15 times more energy than goes in, we have a Colosseum-sized power plant that costs about 10 billion dollars, requires 850 highly educated and highly priced engineers and researchers and produces 1.5 kilowatts of heat, which can be converted to 300 watts of electricity, for example, with the help of modern thermoelectric cells.

So we only need 280 scientists and a few billion dollars of investment to produce enough fusion power for one light bulb, or for five LED lights! Magnificent!

Of course, powerful laser light is the most expensive and simple heat (=the wished end product of NIF) the cheapest and least valuable form of energy on our planet. If you take a square metre of thin, black plastic costing 5 eurocents and spread it into the sun you can collect more heat than the NIF would produce, if it some day achieved its goal of getting out 15 times more energy than what goes in.

If NIF achieves this goal, the electricity produced by it will only be about ten billion times or a thousand billion per cent more expensive than our current grid power.

At the moment we are still very far from this goal. During 2007-2013 the facility has once been able to extract 15 kilojoules of energy from one fuel pellet, by only delivering 10 kilojoules of energy inside the pellet. Five kilojoules of energy is not very much, because it was – again – in the form of heat and not in the form of electricity. If 30 per cent of this 5 kilojoules could be converted to electric power, this would provide enough electricity for one 80-watt light bulb for almost 17 seconds.

So we are not yet very close of the final goal of NIF providing continuous power for five lightbulbs. There is a great difference between lighting five light bulbs permanently and in keeping one light bulb lit for 17 seconds during a period of 300 million seconds.

And, of course, if we also take into account all the conversion losses we should note that the total energy consumption of the lasers during the experiment was 2 megajoules instead of 10 kilojoules. So in reality the consumption of energy was 200 times more than the production.

I have met numerous nuclear experts who consider themselves rational, empirically oriented scientists but who have been able to convince themselves that it is next to impossible to reduce the costs of wind or solar power so much that it becomes economically feasible without subsidies. At the same time most of them believe that fusion is one day going to provide the final answer to the world's energy problems (!).

In other words: a difference of thirty per cent is something impossible, something that just cannot be bridged, but a difference of a thousand billion per cent (if the goal of NIF is achieved, which has not yet happened!) is nothing. Sounds most scientific to me.

But... what if there are astounding technical and scientific breakthroughs that we cannot yet imagine, but which will change everything, after fifty years or so?

This, of course, is theoretically possible. But consider two facts.

The smallest *natural* fission reactor we know of was a few metres across. It existed in Gabon when the earth was younger and natural uranium contained a larger percentage of the easily fissile isotope 235. Since then, its share has declined to 0.7 per cent because it has a half-life of 710 million years, while the less easily fissile uranium 238 has a half-life of 4.6 billion years.

How big are the smallest known natural fusion reactors?

They are so-called red dwarf stars, which are a few tens of thousands of times larger than the planet earth. We know that a planet that is only a few thousand times heavier than the earth does not ignite as a star, even if it mostly consists of hydrogen and helium, the elements required for fusion.

In other words, the smallest natural fusion reactor is approximately a million million million million times larger than the smallest natural fission reactor. Should this tell us something? I think this implies that making a fusion reactor is more difficult than making a fission reactor.

The other point to consider is that Iceland is trying to develop geothermal energy based on supercritical steam, or steam heated to 454 degrees Celsius. If they succeed in this, each geothermal hole will produce 5-10 times more electricity than before. However, there are vast technical problems because it is very difficult to handle water that has been heated to 454 degrees Celsius.

Engineers dreaming about fusion power have to raise the temperature of their mixture of deuterium and tritium not to hundreds or even hundreds of thousands of degrees Celsius, but to 150 million degrees Celsius, meaning 150,000,000 degrees instead of 454.

I would advise the governments to concentrate their resources on the projects that are only aiming at 454 degrees!

ITER and NIF should be re-classified as churches. Temples of a religious sect known as Fusion's Witnesses, or something like that. Fusion research laboratories are places for worshipping Nuclear Energy as the Divine, Cosmic Light. As the Cosmic Love that fills the whole universe.

However, they do not—and they never will—have anything to do with the practical production of electricity for the people, except that fission and fusion still eat the majority of the world's governmental research grants for research aiming to develop new forms of energy not based on fossil fuels. In the USA, for example, their share of federal research funding for non-fossil fuel energy is still a whopping 85 per cent.

These funds would be much better used in other fields of research like solar and wind energy, geothermal energy and bioenergy, which have this far received much smaller amounts of research and development money from the world's governments.

8

Do We Really Need Nuclear Power?

Many people still say that we need nuclear power to prevent disastrous global warming. According to them nuclear power plants are the only realistic and feasible means of producing large amounts of electric power without fossil fuels: renewable energies are either too expensive or too unreliable. Windmills do not provide power when the wind is not blowing and solar power plants only produce power when the sun is shining.

These notions were important thirty years ago and they still had some relevance three years ago but almost everything has changed, since then.

The average cost of constructing a new nuclear power plant (per megawatt) has increased six-fold while the cost of installing wind turbines has been reduced by ten or twelve times. Because of this, the average price of wind power is now less than that of nuclear power.

Even more importantly, this trend is not likely to stop, in the near future. After Fukushima nuclear power plants will be forced to construct at least some defences against tsunamis and hurricane storm surges. It may be that in some countries nuclear companies will no longer be allowed to construct their facilities on the most vulnerable sites like coastal flatlands, less than fifty metres above the sea level.

This will increase the price of nuclear power. If nuclear power companies have to guard the reactors and cooling ponds against terrorist strikes, this will further add to their production costs. If they are forced to pay insurance fees—like all the other companies have to do—the price of nuclear power will increase further. If they have to do something for the used nuclear fuel (very radioactive) and dismantle the used nuclear reactors (also very radioactive) there will be more costs. And so on, and so forth.

At the same time the growing size of the windmills is steadily cutting the average price of wind power. Wind power became, an average, as costly as nuclear power or electricity from gas-fired power plants when the average size of windmills was about three megawatts. EU's project Upwind has calculated, that the production of wind power will reach the height of its productivity when wind turbines reach the size of 20 megawatts. The largest existing prototypes now have the nominal power of 10 megawatts, but companies in Europe, USA and China are developing even bigger ones.

The development of specialized ships for installing and for the maintenance work of such monster windmills and for laying their cables is also going to reduce the price of marine wind power. Marine wind turbines used to cost two times more per installed watt than windmills erected on land, but the difference is quickly becoming smaller.

A windmill on land typically achieves an average production of 20 or 25 per cent of its nominal capacity, but marine wind turbines installed on floating or permanent platforms on windy marine regions have already achieved 45 or even 50 per cent. Sea Titan, the 10-megawatt monster developed by the American Superconductor Corporation, might get close to 70 per cent. It is expected to produce approximately 6,000 megawatt-hours of electricity per year, when installed on windy sites. This is because its cut-off speed (the wind-speed at which the turbine shuts off, automatically) has been raised to 35 metres per second by a new kind of direct-driven wind turbine design, using large magnets instead of gears.

In the near future, nuclear power could be two or three times more expensive per gigawatt-hour than wind power.

The price of photovoltaic power has dropped by 80 per cent (to one-fifth) in five years, during 2008-2012. Germany and some other European countries, especially Spain and Italy, subsidized the production of solar energy so heavily that the increasing demand made it possible to produce a much longer series of photovoltaic panels. Because of this the average price of photovoltaic cells was cut to half during the years 2008-2010. In 2011, during a single year, it was halved again. In January 2012 photovoltaic power in India became for the first time cheaper than power from diesel generators. The price of photovoltaic power was 8.8 rupees per kilowatt-hour and the price of electricity generated by diesel generators 17 rupees per kilowatt-hour. Solar power was still almost two times more expensive than the electricity generated by coal in large thermal power plants, but it was, for the first time, the cheapest form of electric power in most areas outside the national electric grid.

These trends have continued, since then. In February 2014 the cheapest available crystalline silicon solar panels only cost euro 0.45 per watt and the cheapest inverters converting the direct current to alternative current euro 0.10 per watt. Installation costs varied a lot, but for example in Germany, many companies offered prices around euro

0.11 per watt. With this level of expenditure, solar power will already be cheaper than coal power in areas that receive a lot of sunlight.

According to some predictions the price of solar panels will only decrease something like 6 per cent during the year 2014, but soon after this there will be at least one more crash due to changes in the production of solar grade silicon.

Solar grade silicon used to cost around USD 80 and consume 200 kilowatt-hours of energy per kilogram, but the Chinese manufacturer JACO has now started to sell it with only USD 15 per kilogram. JACO's manufacturing process only requires 15 kilowatt-hours of energy to make a kilogram of solar-grade silicon. JACO says that it can soon sell very pure and crystallized silicon with less than 10 USD/kilograms, which has forced all other manufacturers of solar grade to upgrade their own production processes. According to Cambridge University, this will probably force the price down to less than USD 8 and the consumption of energy to less than 10 kilowatt-hours per kilo, during the next few years.

The reduced price of silicon will also benefit the companies manufacturing low-concentration photovoltaic (LCPV) technologies. High-concentration photovoltaic systems use parabolic mirrors or Fresnel lenses to concentrate power from 500 to 2,500 times to small multi-junction solar cells that contain several different layers of rare semi-conducting materials. Low-concentration photovoltaics, on the other hand, only concentrates sunlight from 2 to 100 times and uses ordinary silicon solar panels. For instance, the US company Cogenra started to sell whole LCPV modules with USD 0.50 (or euro 0.35) per watt in spring 2014. They will probably reduce the price further when they can get solar grade silicon with USD 8-10 per kilogram.

The Finnish non-governmental organization CED is currently trying to find a manufacturer that would be interested in producing silicon panels that are capable of withstanding a concentration of 10-20 suns and which could be used in connection with 30 square metre mini-heliostatic solar concentrators designed by the Finnish company SolarFire Concentration Oy.

It would probably be possible to make a wood- or bamboo-framed artisanal 30 square metre concentrator with only 100 USD, if the hard parts were manufactured as assembly kits in a large series in a modern factory, and the rest would be done by India's extremely skilled village artisans. Flat mirrors now only cost about USD 3-5 per square metre! With a small LCPV solar panel costing another 100 USD or so, such a small heliostatic concentrator might be able to produce up to 6 kilowatts of electricity.

It is important to realize, that all this has been achieved without any truly major technological breakthroughs. We are still talking about "old-fashioned" crystalline silicon photovoltaic cells. The most important difference has been, that the production has achieved a much larger scale than before.

Many companies are developing ways to produce photovoltaic cells by printing them outside a vacuum. Some of them are developing roll-on-roll processors of thin-film photovoltaic cells that operate somewhat like paper mills. Others are planning systems that would operate like the printing presses that now produce books, newspapers and magazines. When this kind of advanced production systems become a reality, the price of photovoltaic power will drop far below the price of coal power, not to say anything about nuclear electricity.

In the long run the various high concentration photovoltaic technologies (HCPV) might also be able to produce very cheap solar electricity. For example, IBM has been able to produce 400,000 watts of electricity from one square metre of solar cells by concentrating the sunlight to 2,400 times of its normal intensity. Boeing Spectrolab is already selling its HCPV cells with USD 0.2 per watt and it has promised considerable further price reductions within a short period of time.

Solar thermal is another contender. According to Solar Fire Concentration Oy, it would be possible to produce, in India, 60 square-metre heliostatic solar power plants producing about 40 kilowatts of power in the form of relatively hot steam (200 degrees Celsius) and only costing about 3,500 or 4,000 USD, including a modern steam engine capable of transforming 10 per cent of the heat energy into electricity. The less hot steam could be used to run absorption fridges and direct-driven water pumps. After this the steam could still be used for cooking and to heat the houses whenever there is a need for heating energy.

A Renewed Role for Hydropower

What comes to price nuclear power obviously will not be able to compete with even the currently existing solar and wind power technologies, not to say anything about the solar and wind technologies that will be available for us after five or ten years.

But what about reliability?

Back-up power has long been seen as the main problem of wind and solar power. Where does the power come from when the wind does not blow or the sun does not shine?

One way of solving the problem is to construct large super-grids, consisting of High Voltage Direct Current or HVDC transmission lines. Since they use direct current, they are less vulnerable to geomagnetically induced direct current spikes that can be generated for example by solar storms or nuclear detonations. Above all, they can transport huge amounts of power for thousands of kilometres with relatively small losses. HVDC transmission lines will make it possible to transfer solar power from areas where the sun is still shining to areas where it has already set, and from areas where the sun has already risen to places which are still covered by night. Similarly, they enable us to import wind power from several different marine regions situated very far from each other. This is important, because the winds blowing over different seas tend to rise and die according to a different schedule.

However, this is not the only possible solution, because there are at least two practical and affordable ways to store solar and wind power: the pumped storage power plants and heat storage based on pressurized steam.

Nuclear power plants and large thermal power plants use steam turbines that require supercritical steam, steam heated to 454 degrees Celsius. Maintaining a heat storage for this kind of power plants is not economical because it is not possible to store supercritical heat for a long time and molten salt is thus required. Heat losses increase very rapidly when the temperatures rise.

Steam engines, however, can make electric power with 200-degree Celsius steam, which can be stored relatively easily and economically and without rapid and massive losses of heat. If aerogels, the new superinsulators—0.3 per of which is silica and 99.7 per cent of which is air—become more affordable it will become even easier to store power-generating capacity in steam. One centimetre of the best aerogels has the same heat insulation value as 12 centimetres of polystyrene. Many Chinese companies have doubled or tripled the insulation value of their conventional insulation materials without making them too expensive by adding small amounts of silica aerogels in them.

In pumped storage plants water is pumped upstream to a reservoir when there is extra power. When there is a need for extra power producing capacity, the gates are opened and the water is run through large hydroturbines.

The method has some very clear benefits. The most important is that only 15 per cent of the electricity is lost in the process, much less than for example when the power would be used to produce hydrogen. Eighty-five per cent of the power consumed when the water was pumped upstream can be "taken back" when the same water is run downstream, through the hydroturbines. When more power is needed, the power-producing capacity of a hydropower plant can be raised from zero to 1,000 megawatts in 12 seconds.

We only have 127 gigawatts (127,000 megawatts) of specialized pumped storage power plants in the world. However, we have a huge number of ordinary hydroelectricity: dams, hydroturbines and reservoirs.

The maximum power-producing capacity of the world's currently existing hydropower plants is 1,100 gigawatts. Their average power, however, is only 400 gigawatts. Most hydropower plants run on less than full capacity for most of the year, because the flow of the rivers fluctuates a lot. In the rainy season there is more water in the rivers than during the dry season.

This means, that the existing reservoirs and hydropower plants could also be used as pumped storage power plants with minimal investment, simply by pumping the water up and down with extra solar and wind power, over and over again. This would already give us up to 700,000 megawatts of extra back-up power.

"If we need more, we should find ways of equipping the already existing hydropower plants or those that will be constructed in the future with larger turbines, or learn how to install a larger number of parallel turbines in each hydropower plant.

The present reservoirs behind large dams higher than one hundred metres already contain more than 6,000 cubic kilometres of water. Let's assume, as a thought experiment, that we would transform all these reservoirs to pumped-storage hydropower so that all this water could be discharged through hydroturbines during one night of ten hours. This would mean that when needed, these installations could produce 170,000 gigawatts of electricity during a ten-hour period, almost one hundred times more than humanity's present consumption of electricity. During the next day the water could be pumped back with solar electricity.

Of course, we will never need this much back-up power. But this kind of thought experiment shows that even a minuscule part of our present hydropower capacity would provide us with more than enough reserve power-production capacity, if we transform it to pumped-storage hydropower."

If we need more, we can equip the existing hydropower plants with larger turbines. Or we can install a larger number of parallel turbines on each hydropower plant. This way our already existing dam and reservoir arsenal should be able to provide us with thousands of gigawatts of back-up power, which is already much more than enough.

Because of the freshwater crises, most of the world's governments are still planning to construct new dams and reservoirs, to reduce the percentage of rainwater lost as runoff into the sea during the rainy season(s). Most of these dams will be planned so, that they will also produce electric power.

The industry dreams of doubling the global production of hydropower. This goal is likely to be far too ambitious, because many of the planned reservoirs would drown densely populated agricultural lands and displace large numbers of people. Many of the planned dams also drowned forests and peatland areas, which means that they would probably generate large methane emissions from the biomass decaying at the bottom, in anoxic conditions. Above all, dams and reservoirs tend to act as sediment traps, which is one of the main reasons for the sinking of river deltas and adjoining river valleys. A clear majority of the world's large river deltas are sinking, often with a speed of several centimetres per year. If the sea level rises 2 - 5 metres during the next one hundred years while the delta sinks by four metres, the effective sea level rise will be from six to nine metres. The problem can be somewhat reduced with sludge gates installed in the dams, but they may not be enough.

Whenever new dams and reservoirs are built, it would make sense to construct them so, that they can also act as pumped storage power plants and provide large quantities of back-up power for our future energy systems.

Sodium batteries may also become a viable option for

storing large amounts of electricity. Our most efficient batteries now use lithium, because lithium ions are so small that you can store 0.24 kilowatt-hours of electricity for each kilogram of weight. Besides this, the best lithium batteries can be recharged an astonishing 7,000 times. Unfortunately, the mining and refining of lithium consumes a lot of energy and produces toxic waste, and battery-grade lithium hydroxide costs about euro 7,500 per ton. Battery-grade sodium sulphate would only cost about euro 120 per ton and consume much less energy. The main problem has been to find suitable materials for the anods of sodium batteries, but many companies and research institutes have been looking for a solution and have already published promising results.

In other words, we do not really need nuclear power for any constructive purposes.

Can Nuclear Power Ever be Cost-Effective?

The public discussion is still focusing on whether wind and solar power can become affordable alternatives. In these sectors the development has been rapid and the prospects for further improvement are very exciting.

The question about the economic feasibility of nuclear power has received much less attention, which is strange, keeping in mind that while during the last thirty years the price of wind power has been reduced by ten or twelve times the average price of nuclear power plants (for each megawatt of capacity) has increased six-fold.

Finland's Olkiluoto 3 is an excellent reference point. The Finnish nuclear power company Teollisuuden Voima paid 3.2 billion euros for the 1,600 Mw reactor, but the final cost for Areva, the French manufacturer of the reactor, will be at least 9 billion euros and possibly more. Besides this, delays in construction have already cost Teollisuuden Voima 1.6 billion euros, according to its own, published statement. If the losses of Teollisuuden Voima and the actual costs of Areva are counted together, the real price of the reactor may finally amount to something like 13 or 14 billion euros, when the facility finally begins to operate.

The two 1,500 Mw nuclear reactors of Britain's Hinkley Point C power plant are expected to cost 19 billion euros or 9.5 billion euros per reactor, but the final figure could be much larger if there are delays or unexpected problems, which have been the norm in nuclear industry. The project would not be economically feasible without massive government subsidies. The two reactors are expected to produce 26 Twh of electricity, annually, and the British government has guaranteed a minimum price of 109.4 euros per Mwh for the company building the reactors for a period of 35 years.

The average wholesale price for electricity in Britain has varied between 40 and 50 euros per megawatt-hour, which is 69-59 euros less than the price guaranteed by the government. If the price difference remains similar, the British government will be committed to paying between 50 and 63 billion euros as government subsidies for Hinkley Point C during the next 35 years.

As M.V. Ramana has noted, the economic prospects concerning the fourth-generation nuclear power plants are even dimmer. The only large fourth-generation production reactor which has ever been built, the Superphenix of France, only produced 7.9 billion kilowatt-hours of electricity during its eleven years of existence. Thus, its average power production only amounted to 6.6 per cent of its nominal power during the operations and to much less if we also included the construction period in our calculations.

Since fourth-generation nuclear power plants would also be much more expensive than ordinary nuclear power plants, it is hard to see how they could provide us with cheap electricity. If a Superphenix built according to present safety standards had a two times higher megawatt-cost than the Hinkley Point C reactors and produced as much electricity as Superphenix did, its electricity might cost something like 5 euros per kilowatt-hour, roughly one hundred times more than the electricity produced by photovoltaic panels in North Europe (according to the price level that prevailed in June 2013).

It is possible that major improvements in the performance of the fourth-generation nuclear power plants could be achieved within half a century or so if the governments and their tax-payers were willing to invest a few hundred or a few thousand billion more euros into nuclear research and development. But if we only focus on the already existing technologies and what they can do, this comparison—Superphenix vs the present kinds of photovoltaic panels in Europe—should perhaps be seen as the actual state-of-the-art of these two competing technologies.

Collateral Damage: Nuclear Power and Particulate Matter

As mentioned in the first chapter, nuclear power does not necessarily cause very many direct deaths. We do not yet know with any certainty, whether uranium mines, nuclear accidents and routine emissions from nuclear power plants and the recycling facilities cause an average a thousand or tens of thousands of deaths per year. The figure of course cannot be higher than 80,000 even if most cancers in the world were caused by radioactive exposures—simply because only 1 per cent of our total radioactive exposure is caused by the nuclear industries.

However, nuclear power has caused a very large number of indirect deaths by three different mechanisms.

One of them I have already discussed in detail in the fourth chapter of this book. It seems that because of nuclear power it has been almost forbidden to have a serious discussion on what should be done to eliminate different unnecessary radioactive exposures. If the various radioactive exposures were seen as a problem, as something dangerous, also the popularity of nuclear energy might suffer. This has, in a way, increased the damage done by nuclear industry 100-fold or so.

Another problem has been, that the proponents of nuclear power have presented it as a solution to the particulate problem.

As mentioned before, particulate pollution is a very serious health issue. According to a semi-official analysis of a vast amount of research literature, published in the prestigious medical journal *Lancet* in 2010, particulate pollution may already cause about seven million premature deaths, each year. Even this may be a gross underestimate. Many scientists believe that the real figure could be at least two times higher.

Air pollution annually kills about 500,000 people in the European Union member countries, which have about 500 million people. The average air pollution mortality among the seven billion people of the world is most probably higher than in the European Union, because most of the people living outside Europe are exposed to much higher levels of pollution.

So the issue is real, but it is absolutely preposterous to claim that it could be solved with nuclear power. At least 50 or 60 per cent of all deaths related to particulate pollution are most probably caused by pollution released inside people's homes by highly polluting traditional cooking stoves using solid biomass fuels or mineral coal. Most of the rest is caused by the particulate pollution released into the outside air by polluting cooking stoves, campfires, forest fires, cars and lorries and by the annual burning of billions of tons of crop residues in the fields.

There is nothing that can be done for these emissions by constructing nuclear power. For example in India, only 0.2 million households cook with electric power. About 180 million households use traditional or slightly improved cooking stoves burning solid fuels, 7 million use kerosene, 72 million LPG, 4.5 million biogas and 0.5 million solar cookers.

The energy of electric power is roughly one hundred times more expensive than the energy available in the form of the cheapest solid biofuels, so even if we are able to produce a larger amount of expensive electricity, it would not do much for reducing the particulate pollution problem. Some wealthier people might shift from LPG or kerosene to electricity, but this would have almost no impact on particulate matter emissions because LPG and kerosene are also very clean-burning fuels.

Of course, the pollutants from coal-fired power plants also cause a large number of premature deaths, probably around 100,000 per year. It might be theoretically possible to reduce this death toll by increasing the production of nuclear power, but only if the official estimates about the cancer and health risks of radiation have been roughly correct and not much too low.

Because of the nuclear debate the mostly rightist, centrist and sometimes social democratic parties that have been pushing for nuclear power have imagined that by doing this they are already doing something to reduce particulate pollution. In other words, instead of doing something for the real causes for the problem, they have concentrated in pushing for new nuclear power plants and in using the air pollution issue as an argument in support of nuclear electricity.

On the other hand, the mostly green, leftist and social democratic and sometimes centrist parties that have opposed nuclear power have also ignored the issue of particulate pollution because they have been conditioned to consider it primarily as an argument for nuclear power plants, used by their most important opponents.

Because of this nobody has been passionately interested in doing something for the particulate matter emissions, even if 90 per cent of the problem could have been solved almost without cost, by finding better uses for crop residues and by distributing 400 million top-lit updraft micro-gasifiers or TLUD cooking stoves for the world's poorest families with a subsidized cost. TLUD gasifiers are simple cooking stoves that can be manufactured by 3-5 euros but which can burn any kind of small biomass by 100-300 times smaller soot and particulate matter emissions than the traditional cooking stoves. For example, Saibashkar Nakka Reddy and Priyadarshini Karve have developed numerous excellent models.

In a way at least 200 million people and possibly many

more have died during the last twenty-five years as collateral damage of the war against or for nuclear power. Even though the pro-nuclear forces must bear a greater part of the blame, the anti-nuclear camp has been almost equally guilty in neglecting a hugely important public health issue. In the future, no matter what happens for the world's nuclear power programmes, both anti-nuclear and pro-nuclear people should also do something for the particulate pollution, instead of claiming that this problem will be automatically solved either by nuclear power or by renewable electricity.

However, there is also a third indirect way through which nuclear power has probably caused a very large number of deaths.

Circadian Rhythms, or Why is it Better to Adjust to a Solar than to a Nuclear Economy?

All life on earth has adjusted to a 24-hour-day during the billions of years there has been some kind of life on our planet. Humans also have a large number of natural rhythms that operate in 24-hour cycles. It seems that they influence all kinds of things in our bodies: the strength of immune responses and inflammatory reactions, the excretion of many kinds of hormones, and so on.

It also seems that it is very dangerous to interfere with your circadian rhythms. Shift workers have a multiple risk of getting into a lethal accident. This is no joke, because accidents kill about five million people, every year, one quarter of this in traffic accidents.

Besides this, shift workers have a 50 or 60 per cent higher than normal risk of getting a stroke and a two times higher risk of a heart attack. Even more surprisingly, female shift workers have a 60 per cent higher risk of getting breast cancer, and it seems that shift work also increases the risk of many other cancers, including colorectal and prostate cancer. Further research may reveal more connections between other types of cancers and shift work.

It really looks as if an erratic schedule of sleeping is able to mess up the rhythms of our immune system so that we become more vulnerable to cancer, cardiovascular disease and accidents. It should be kept in mind that the above mentioned correlations might be under-estimates because in the "control group"—among the non-shift workers—there are also many people who sleep too little and too erratically during the night, because of insomnia, because of shift-work of a spouse, parent or child, because of noise or light pollution, or some other reason.

It would probably be better to adjust our societies to solar rather than nuclear economy.

Solar panels and most solar power plants can only produce power during the day, when the sun is shining. This is often seen as the most serious drawback of solar power.

Nuclear power plants, however, have the opposite problem. They have to keep producing the same amount of electricity, through the night and day. Their power-production cannot be increased or decreased without great difficulties and extra risks.

When the first nuclear power plants started to operate in my own country, Finland, this was a problem because people generally want to sleep at night. Since then the government and the industries have actively forced the whole Finnish society to adjust to nuclear economy. Night-time lighting has been expanded and the government has passed legislation that keeps many shops open throughout the night. The amount of three-shift labour has been increased, to a great extent, and people have been encouraged to use night-time electric heating in winter, to store heat for the day. In spite of all this, there is still much more demand for electricity during the day than during the night! You can try to fight people's circadian rhythms—and kill several people along the way—but it will be an uphill battle.

Wouldn't it be better to forget nuclear power and adjust to solar economy, instead? This would be easier, because people generally want to sleep during the night.

Some of the doctors and nurses, firemen and police will have to be on duty even at night. But solar economy might bring proper nights and a life largely based on natural circadian rhythms back for the rest of us.

A Small End Note: Are We Still Living in a Dream?

In the 1960s and 1970s the governments and large corporations were dreaming of aeroplanes, trains and ordinary freight and passenger ships powered by small nuclear reactors. The Ploughshare programme of the US government looked for constructive and peaceful uses for nuclear weapons. It seriously inspected the possibility of using nuclear bombs to excavate canals and the basements of large buildings, to dig mines and to open natural gas wells.

The US government financed, in 1957-65, a project called Orion, which aimed at developing nuclear pulse propulsion for manned, interplanetary space flights to Mars and to the moons of Jupiter and Saturn. The nuclear spaceship would have been equipped with a pusher plate, behind which a long series of nuclear detonations would take place. The shock wave of the explosions would hit the plate and push the space ship towards the desired direction.

The project also designed, on paper, an interstellar version of the nuclear spaceship. The interstellar SuperOrion would have required 25 million megaton-class nuclear bombs to reach Alpha Centauri in 150 years, thousands of times more than humanity's combined nuclear arsenal at the height of the Cold War. SuperOrion would have flown straight through the Alpha Centauri system. It would not have been able to stop, not to say anything about turning back and returning to earth.

The radioactive fallout from the explosions pushing SuperOrion towards Alpha Centauri would have been ejected into the opposite direction, towards our own solar system, in the form of plasma, electrically charged particles, many of which would have been captured by the magnetic field of our home planet and rained down from the sky over the oceans and continents.

In 1976 the British Interplanetary Society developed an unmanned version of the same idea, called Daedalus. Daedalus would have flown to Barnard's star in 49 years with the assistance of 30,000 million very small nuclear bombs.

In the 1950s nuclear scientists predicted that power metres would soon become obsolete and unnecessary because electricity provided by nuclear reactors would be so cheap that it would no longer make economic sense to measure how much of it each customer was using.

Edward Teller, one of the fathers of the hydrogen bomb, said that humans have now become stellar architects. Teller commented that humans were now able to make stars and were no longer restricted by the sizes and characteristics of the existing stars. According to Teller: "We now have to decide what kind of stars we want to make."

Scientists proposed that the US Army would include Atomic Bazookas—portable rocket launchers firing small nuclear warheads in close combat situations—into their arsenal, as well as nuclear bombers powered with open nuclear furnaces. The open furnaces had enabled the crew to replace the fuel rods themselves, during the flight. Nuclear scientists also proposed that the US government should develop "Cabasa Howitzers", asymmetrical nuclear detonations firing huge balls of million-degrees-hot plasma towards enemy countries.

US generals were less than convinced by these proposals and even in the civil sectors it is now understood that most of the mentioned proposals had been outright insane and that some would probably have destroyed the human species, had they been carried out according to the original plans. The plans about nuclear aeroplanes were killed when the world-famous US physicist W.R. Bussard calculated, that engineers making such planes would be forced to use so highly enriched nuclear fuels that the whole aeroplane —plus the crew and passengers—would be vaporized 30 seconds after a malfunction would occur in the reactor's cooling system.

We no longer hear about space-ships using nuclear-pulse propulsion, nor about atomic cars and helicopters. Nobody wants to excavate the basements of apartment buildings with nuclear weapons, and mines and canals are still dug by less extreme means.

Most of us would now admit, that the nuclear dreams of the 1950s, 60s and 70s were wildly exaggerated, that they were a part of an era during which we were hypnotized by our own scientific and technological progress and by the dream of excessive wealth and well-being brought for us by nuclear energy, power too cheap to measure. We have also noticed that the electricity-producing utilities are still sending power bills to us. In Finland power has not become too cheap to measure. On the contrary: the price of electricity has risen with the average speed of 6 per cent per year during the last thirty years, in spite of massive investments in nuclear power.

However, most people would probably also say that it was then, it is now history, we have now woken up. That we are now acting in a more rational and responsible way.

But...have we really woken up, or are we still dreaming?

Are we, or at least some of us, still so obsessed with the nuclear dream, that we still refuse to wake up and face the hard realities?

We no longer have three million Hiroshimas of nuclear weapons. But the world's nuclear arsenal still amounts to 80,000 Hiroshima bombs and we are still producing electricity with nuclear power.

A few years before Fukushima, Japan's national nuclear research institute proposed that Japan should initiate the mass-manufacturing of tiny, lithium-cooled nuclear reactors. These so-called Rapid-L reactors would have been installed in the basements of large office buildings or apartment houses. Each would have provided the power for a single building. They had contained fuel in which the uranium 235 content would have been raised to 60 per cent, and they would have used lithium 6 as their emergency coolant. In other words, every one of the thousands or tens of thousands of Rapid-L mini-reactors had contained the ingredients for making vast, two- or three-staged Super-Bombs, like Czar Bomba.

After Fukushima it is psychologically unthinkable to consider installing small nuclear reactors in basements in Japan, but before the accident the plan was taken very seriously. And even today almost every day a nuclear physicist somewhere puts forward a new concept of a new kind of nuclear reactor that would be totally safe, that would not produce dangerous contaminants, that would have a hundred times better energy return on energy investment than our present reactors, that would be able to produce several times more energy than there is in a pile of coal bigger than the earth, and that would probably also produce electricity too cheap to measure. Most of these new Supersafe Reactors would use fuels that can be used as such to make nuclear weapons.

So have we woken up or are we still dreaming?

Will the future generations, if there are any, see a difference between our present nuclear dreams and the ones that dominated the 1960s and 1970s? Or will Rapid-L, the Integrated Fast Reactor, the EPR and the LFTR look, in their eyes, similar to nuclear aeroplanes, Atomic Bazookas and the excavation of the basements of apartment buildings with nuclear detonations?

Selected References

Nuclear weapons are above all fire bombs: Lynn, Eden: *Whole World on Fire, Organizations, Knowledge and Nuclear Weapons Devastation*, Cornell University Press, 2004.

Skyscrapers are planned to resist 250-kilometre-per hour winds without toppling: Eden, ibid.

The detonation of a Hiroshima bomb-sized nuclear weapon at Manhattan would create 600-kilometres-per hour super-hurricane winds blowing from the perimeter towards the firestorm: Goldman, Bruce: Nightmare in Manhattan, *New Scientist*, March 18, 2006.

The costs of the US nuclear weapons programme: Rhodes, Richard: *Arsenals of Folly, the Making of the Nuclear Arms Race*, Simon & Schuster, 2007.

Soot produced by a small nuclear war causing a global famine: Robock, Alan and Toon, Owen B.: Local Nuclear War, Global Suffering, *Scientific American*, January 2010.

Gorbachev-Reagan Scenario: Rhodes, Richard: *Arsenals of Folly, the Making of the Nuclear Arms Race*, Simon & Schuster, 2007: Reagan, Ronald: *An American Life*, Simon & Schuster, 1990.

The fate of K-129: Sewell, Kenneth and Richmond, Clint: *Red Star Rogue, The Untold Story of a Soviet Submarine's Nuclear Strike Attempt on the US*, Pocket Star Books, 2006; Weir, Gary E. and Boyne, Walter J.: *Rising Tide, the Untold Story of the Russian Submarines that Fought the Cold War*, Basic Books, 2003; Project Jennifer, Hughes Glomar Explorer, Federation of American Scientists, March 8, 1999, http://www.fas.org/irp/program/collect/jennifer.htm.

The Nazi scientists were only able to enrich the uranium 235 content from 0.7 to 1.5 per cent in one gram of uranium hexafluoride: Baggott, Jim: *Atomic, The First War of Physics*, Icon Books, 2009.

What is meant by fourth-generation nuclear reactors: see the website of GIF (Generation-4 International Forum): www.gen-4.org/GIF/About/index.htm.

The enrichment rate of breeder reactor fuel, see for instance: Columbia State Universityn palkitut Hyperphysics-verkkosivut, Department of Physics and Astronomy of the Columbia State University, hyperphysics + fast breeder reactors; Kambe, M. et al: Rapid Operator-free Fast Reactors Combined with Thermoelectric Power Conversion System, *Journal of Power and Energy*, 218: 335-343, 2004.

Uranium fuel containing 10 or 12 per cent of uranium 233 can be used to make a nuclear weapon, see for instance: Forsberg, C.W., Hopper, C.M., Richter, J.L., Vantine, H.C.: *Definition of Weapons-Usable Uranium-233*, Oak Ridge National Laboratory, Los Alamos National Laboratory, Lawrence Livermore National Laboratory, March 1998.

Making nuclear bombs from uranium containing 20 per cent of uranium 235: Glaser, Alexander and Hippel, Frank von: Thwarting Nuclear Terrorism, *Scientific American*, February, 2006; Allison, Graham: *Nuclear Terrorism, the Risks and Consequences of the Ultimate Disaster*, Constable, 2005.

Different forms of plutonium and the use of reactor-grade plutonium in manufacturing nuclear weapons: Garwin, Richard L.: Reactor-Grade Plutonium Can be Used to Make Powerful and Reliable Nuclear Weapons, August 26, 1998, http://www.fas.org/rlg/980826-pu.htm; DOE Facts: Additional Information Concerning Underground Nuclear Weapon Test of Reactor-Grade Plutonium, US Department of Energy, Office of Public Affairs, http://www.ccnr.org/plute_bomb.html; Physical, Nuclear and Chemical Properties of Plutonbium, IEER Fact Sheet, http://www.ieer.org/fctsheet/pu-props.html.

The Castle series of nuclear experiments (and other nuclear weapons tests): There is now an enormous supply of public material, but one extremely accessible site is: http://nuclearweapon-archive.org/USA/tests/castle.html. When looking for information about other experiments of the USA or of nuclear experiments conducted by other countries, just change the name of the country and series (of experiments).

Hydrogen-Uranium bombs: Rotblat, Joseph: The Hydrogen-Uranium Bomb, *Bulletin of the Atomic Scientists*, May 1955, 171-172. All the old numbers of the Bulletin are now available on the net and constitute an excellent source of information about nuclear technology.

The assessment of EPA (Environmental Protection Agency) of the USA of radiation risks: Environmental Protection Agency: Radiation Risks and Realities, Understanding Radiation in Your Life, Your World, EPA, 2007.

A summary of 730 Russian, Ukrainian and Belorussian studies about the health impact of Chernobyl, including a summary of the methodology and results of each study: Busby, C.C. and Yablokov, A.V.: Chernobyl 20 Years On: Health Effects of the Chernobyl Accident, European Committee on Radiation Risk (ECRR), Brussels, 2006. Available as a free e-book. ECRR is a network of serious scientists who are concerned with the possibility that we have seriously underestimated the risks related to certain types of radioactive exposure. Their points and the mentioned 730 Russian, Belorussian and Ukrainian studies have been completely ignored by the mainstream of Western nuclear scientists.

Infant mortality in Britain after Chernobyl: Herbert, Ian and Linton, Deborah: Chernobyl Disaster linked to higher rate of infant mortality, http://news.independent.co.uk, March 23, 2006.

The development of infant mortality in India during the years after Chernobyl: Ghoshal, Sumit: One Million Infant Deaths in India from Chernobyl, www.mothersalert.org, April 26, 2000.

Infant mortality in Poland after Chernobyl: The 6.2 per cent rise in infant mortality in Poland after Chernobyl, Wise, July 6, 1990.

The study that "proved" officially that the increase in infant mortality in Bavaria (Germany) after Chernobyl could not have anything to do with Chernobyl: Grosche, B. et al: Perinatal Mortality in Bavaria, Germany, After the Chernobyl Nuclear Accident, *Radiation and Environmental Biophysics*, 36, 1432-2099, July, 1997.

Smoking in China during the Ming and Qing Dynasties: Mann, Charles C.: 1493, *Uncovering the New World Columbus Created*, Alfred A. Knopf, New York, 2011.

The comparision of radioactive exposures of a lung X-rays and smoking: EPA, 2007, ibid; Fusrap Fact Sheet, Radiation at Fusrap Sites, US Army Corps of Engineers, Buffalo District, April, 1998; University of Iowa Hospitals & Clinics, Cancer Prevention: What You Need to Know, Radiation Exposure: The Facts vs Fiction; Toivonen, Harri et al: Tapaus Litvinenko, Alara Nro 1, 2007, Suomen Säteilyturvakeskus, 2007; American Cancer Society: General Questions and Comments on Radiation Risk; Radioactive Exposure due to Smoking Could be Less than Thought,

Destination Sante.com, January 6, 2009.

Tobacco-related cancer and polonium 210: Radford, Edward P. and Hunt, Vilma R.: Polonium-210: A Volatile Radioelement in Cigarettes, *Science*, 143: 247-249, January 17, 1964; Muggli, Monique E.: Waking a Sleeping Giant: The Tobacco Industry's Response to the Polonium-210 Issue, *American Journal of Public Health*, 98: 1643-1650, 2008; Rego, Brianna: The Polonium Brief, A Hidden History of Cancer, Radiation and the Tobacco Industry, *Isis*, 100: 453-484, 2009;

Rego, Brianna: Radioactive Smoke, *Scientific American*, January 2011.

The amount of polonium in cigarettes has increased while filters have reduced the amount of chemical carcinogens in tobacco smoke: Marmorstein, Jerome: Lung Cancer: Is the Increasing Incidence Due to Radioactive Polonium in Cigarettes?, *Southern Medical Journal*, 79(2): 145-150, 1986; Hill, C.R.: Polonium-210 in Man, Nature, 208: 423-428, 1965.

Carcinogenic exposures caused by woodfuel smoke in India: CSE: *The State of India's Environment 1984-85, The Second Citizens' Report*, Centre for Science and Environment, New Delhi, 1985.

Cancer in Egyptian Mummies: David, Rosalie A. and Zimmermann, Michael R.: Cancer: An Old Disease, A New Disease or Something in Between?, *Nature Reviews*, Cancer: 10: 728-733, October 2010; Young, Emma: Ancient Afflictions, *New Scientist*, November 9, 2013.

The annual number of lung cancer cases increasing 40-fold between 1920 and 1960 in Britain: Taylor, Peter: *The Smoke Ring, Tobacco, Money and Multinational Politics*, Sphere Books, London, 1984.

Cancers caused by viruses and bacteria: Ewald, Paul W.: *Plague Time, The New Germ Theory of Disease*, Anchor Books, 2000; Ewald, Paul W.: *Evolution of Infectious Disease*, Anchor Books, 1998.

Cancer caused by immunological storms, chronic inflammation and (possibly also) by bone fractures: Agus, David B.: *The End of Illness*, Simon & Schuster, 2011.

Malarial immunosuppression and cancer: Enwere, Ota et al: The host response in malaria and depression of defence against tuberculosis, *Annals of Tropical Medicine and Parasitology*, 93: 669-678; 1999; Greenwood, B.M.: Autoimmune Disease and Parasitic Infections in Nigeria, *Lancet* ii: 380-382.1968.

Sunlight, D-vitamin, health and cancer: The amount of research literature on the subject is increasing by almost ten thousand new studies per year, but for an authoritative general discussion see for example Holick, Michael F.: *The Vitamin D Solution*, Hudson Street Press, 2010.

Tritium emissions by Finnish nuclear power plants: Isomäki, Risto: *Kosminen Rakkaus vai Suuri Saatana*, Into Kustannus, Helsinki, 2009.

Tritium emissions by Indian nuclear power plants and nuclear fuel reprocessing facilities: Ramana, M.V.: *The Power of Promise, Examining Nuclear Energy in India*, Penguin Viking, 2012. Highly recommended, without doubt the best book about nuclear power I have ever read and possibly the best book anybody has ever written about the subject.

The radioactivity of used nuclear fuel and the amount of residual heat generated by the decay of radioactive impurities in nuclear fuel after the reactor shut-down, see for instance: Lipschutz, Ronnie: *Radioactive Waste: Politics, Technology and Risk,* Ballinger Publishing Company, Cambridge (Massachusetts), 1980; Bloemke, J.O. et al: *Projections of Radioactive Wastes to be Generated by the US Nuclear Power Industry*, Oak Ridge National Laboratory, 1974.

The risk of a zirconium fire in a cooling pond: Hui, Zhang: Radiological Terrorism: Sabotage of Spent Fuel Pools, INESAP (International Network of Engineers and Scientists Against Proliferation), 22: 75-78, December 2003; Alvarez, Robert: Nuclear Safety and Terrorism, The Foreign Policy in Focus Project, November 26, 2001; Zirconium. Covering for Fuel Rods, *The New York Times* in verkkosivut, http://query.nytimes.com; Safety and Security of Commercial Spent Nuclear Fuel Storage: Public Report, Board on Radioactive Waste Management, USA, 2006; Wald, Matthew L.: Study Finds Vulnerabilities in Pools of Spent Nuclear Fuel; *The New York Times*, April 7, 2005; Sensintaffar, Edwin L. and Philips, Charles R.: Environmental Impact Resulting from a Fire at a Spent Nuclear Fuel Storage Facility, *International Journal of Nuclear Governance, Economy and Ecology*, Vol. 1, No. 3, 2007.

The assessment that a zirconium fire could release 100 per cent of the Cesium 137 in used nuclear fuel: Travis, R.J., Davis, R.E., Grove, E.J. and Azram, M.A.: *A Safety and Regulatory Assessment of Generic BWR and PWR Permanently Shutdown Nuclear Power Plants*, Brookhaven National Laboratory, Nureg/cr-6451; BL-Nureg-52498, 1997.

Global warming and the melting of ice sheets and methane clathrate fields, see for instance: Isomäki, Risto: *66 Ways to Absorb Carbon and*

Improve the Earth's Reflectivity, from Mad Scientist Solutions to Reasonable Options, available as an ordinary book, as an e-book, as a mobile book (widget or mobi) and as a free pdf-file (www.into-ebooks.com).

Tsunamis caused at the Baltic Sea by the melting of the Fennoscandian ice sheet: Mörner, Nils-Axel: Tsunami Events within the Baltic, Polish Geological Institute Special Papers, 23, 71-76, 2008.

Factors influencing wave height: Massel, Stanislaw R.: *Ocean Surface Waves, Their Physics and Prediction*, Singapore, World Scientific, 1996.

Melting and vaporization points and heats and specific heat capacities of uranium dioxide: International Nuclear Safety Center: Vapor Pressure of Uranium Oxide; International Bio-Analytical Industries, Inc: Physical Constants of Uranium Oxide; Ohse, R.W., Fabelot, J.F., Brumme, G.D. and Kinsman, P.R.: *Vapour Pressure Studies over Liquid Uranium Oxide and Uranium Plutonium Oxide up to 5000 K*, Wiley Online Library, May 5, 2010.

The Michelson-Medlin–Stafford –study about the mortality that could be caused by a dirty bomb made of used nuclear fuel freshly taken out from a nuclear reactor: Nichelson, Scott M., Stafford, Matthew C. and Medlin, Darren D.: *Radiological Weapons of Terror*, Maxwell Air Force Base, A1: Air University Air Command and Staff College, 1999.

The assessment of the American Federation of Scientists about the dangers related to dirty bombs: Testimony of Dr. Henry Kelly, President, Federation of American Scientists, before the Senate Subcommittee on Foreign Relations, March 6, 2002; Levi, M.A. and Kelly, H.C.: Weapons of Mass Disruption, *Scientific American*, November 2002, 77-81.

US planning to create a radioactive death zone in Korea: Hamblin, Jacob Darwin: *Arming Mother Nature: The Birth of Catastrophic Environmentalism*, Oxford University Press, 2013.

Portable bunker-breaker missiles (Deep Digger) and their capacity to penetrate through concrete walls: Levi, Michael: Bunker Buster Bombs, *Scientific American*, August 2004.

The number of armed security guards in US nuclear power plants: Behrens, Carl and Holt, Mark: Nuclear Power Plants: Vulnerability to Terrorist Attack, CRS Report for Congress, Updated February 4, 2005, Congressional Research Service, the Library of Congress.

The assessment that the oxidation of the zirconium cladding of used nuclear fuel rods can release large amounts of cesium 137 already in 600 degrees Celsius: Zhang, Hui, ibid.

The coolant void co-efficient of Indian breeder reactors: Kumar, Ashwin and Ramana, M.V.: The Safety Inadequacies of India's Fast Breeder Reactor, *Bulletin of Atomic Scientists*, July 21, 2009.

The differences between different types of fusion reactors, see for instance: Schmitt, Harrison: *Return to the Moon*, Praxis Publishing, New York, 2006. Schmitt is one of the two people who visited the moon with the last Apollo flight, a former US senator, a fusion researcher in Wisconsin University, and an eager proponent of fusion power.

National Ignition Facility: Jamieson, Valerie: Monsters of the Universe, *New Scientist*, August 28, 2004. Progress in NIF in November 2013: Aron, Jacob: Fusion power inches closer to stardom, *New Scientist*, February 15, 2014.

The price of nuclear-power plants has increased 6-fold: Goodall, Chris: Ten Technologies to Fix Energy and Climate, Green Profile, London, 2008. The expected costs of Hinkley Point C nuclear power plant: Vasama, Tanja: Britannia rakentaa ydinvoimalan, Helsingin Sanomat, October 22, 2013.

The costs and performance of Superphenix: see M.V. Ramana, ibid.

The development of the price of photovoltaic power in India: Marshall, Michael: Panel price crash could spark solar revolution, *New Scientist*, February 4, 2012.

The Lancet study saying that particle pollution now kills seven million people a year: Lim, Stephen S. et al: A Comparative Risk Assessment of Burden of Disease and Injury Attributable to 67 Factors and Risk Factor Clusters in 21 Regions, 1990-2010: A Systematic Analysis for the Global Burden of Disease Study 2010; *Lancet*, Vol. 380 (No. 9859), 2224-2260. Kirk Smith's Studies: *The State of India's Environment 1984-85*, CSE, Delhi, 1985.

Circadian rhythms, cancer, accidents and cardiovascular disease, see for instance: Heikkilä, Riikka: Yötyö voi vaarantaa terveyden, Yle arkisto, Akuutti, October 8, 2002; Coren, Stanley: Daylight Savings Time and Traffic Accidents, *New England Journal of Medicine*, 334: 924-925, April 4, 1996; Agus, David B.: *The End of Illness*, Simon & Schuster, 2011; Zhu, Yong et al: Does the Clock Matter in Prostate Cancer, Cancer Epidemiology, Biomarkers and Prevention, 15:3, January 2006; Rajaratnam, Shantha M.W. et al: Sleep loss and circadian disruption in shift work: Health burden and management, *Medical Journal of Australia*, 199 (8):11-15, 2013.